Support for
Peace of Mind

We really do need to begin with the children to teach peace. And children need teachers and other adults in their lives to model and support their learning. This welcome curriculum is a great resource for those adults.

Marsha S. Blakeway, Adjunct Faculty, School for Conflict Analysis and Resolution, George Mason University

We want our children to master their academics but we equally want them to master being good citizens who care about one another and the world at large. The Peace [of Mind] Program does just that. In an age where bullying has become a major problem, the Program is proactive instead of reactive, thereby eliminating some of those problems before they begin. The Peace [of Mind] Program also offers a safe haven for learners of different modalities to thrive in a safe environment.

Jackie Snowden, Assistant Principal, Lafayette Elementary School, Washington D.C.

I believe that if there were a program like Linda Ryden's Peace of Mind in each elementary school across America, we would likely see a wholesale reduction in bullying and juvenile crime. The value that the Peace of Mind program provides to the Lafayette community is immeasurable.

Sam Frumkin, parent, Lafayette Elementary School Washington DC

This program is invaluable to the growth of our students.

Jared Catapano, Teacher, Lafayette Elementary School, Washington D.C.

The Peace [of Mind] Program has many benefits for students and teachers. First, it gives us common language to use and common experience on which to draw as we work and learn together. Second, students learn to pay attention to their feelings and verbalize emotions, which helps them act more mindfully to themselves and to each other.

Laura Pajor, Reading Specialist, Lafayette Elementary School

Peace [of Mind] class is a reflective opportunity for students in grades Pre-K through 5th grade to practice mindful thinking. The impact of taking a moment to breathe and rest our thoughts, allows students to refocus their attention so that they can be more productive and successful in the classroom.

Jessica Sikking, Teacher, Lafayette Elementary School

Peace of Mind Core Curriculum for Early Childhood

Peace of Mind Core Curriculum for First and Second Grade

Peace of Mind Core Curriculum for Third to Fifth Grade

www.TeachPeaceofMind.com

Peace of Mind, LLC, Washington, D.C. 20015
www.TeachPeaceofMind.com
Copyright 2016 Linda Ryden

Cover and interior design: Schwa Design Group
Logo: Pittny Creative

ISBN 978-0-9976954-0-3
Library of Congress Control Number: 2016909796

Published 2016

Contents

Introduction

In 2003 I accepted a challenge that radically changed the direction of my life. When I agreed to teach two classes a week in conflict resolution at my local elementary school, I never imagined that it would become a full-time, whole school program. I never imagined that it would become my life's work. I have had the privilege of working with hundreds of kind, funny, thoughtful, loving children. I have been given the chance to learn and teach concepts that come straight from my heart and I have been given the freedom to create and rein-vent and experiment. I wish that every teacher could have these opportunities.

Over the years, many people have asked me how they can start a "peace program" like mine at their school. This curriculum is my attempt to answer those requests and share some of what I have learned over the past twelve years. This curriculum does not represent my whole program but rather a snapshot of what I get to do every year. I teach 25 classes a week for 40 weeks a year. I get to work with the same children week to week from the time they are in first grade until they graduate from 5th grade. But it didn't start out this way.

Twelve years ago I was teaching two classes a week as a volunteer. This program grew very slowly and responded to needs that I saw at my school. The greatest need I saw was for a way to help the children learn how to calm down when they were angry. After several years of teaching conflict resolution I felt frustrated that the kids didn't often use their skills in the heat of the moment. I searched for a way to teach the kids to recognize their feelings before they became overwhelming and to manage their strong feelings. This search led me to mindfulness, which changed my life and, perhaps, the lives of all of the children in my program.

I have found that combining the internal lessons of mindfulness with the external tools we learn in conflict resolution and social emotional learning is powerful. The combination, with mindfulness as the foundation for all of the SEL lessons, is, in my experience, much more effective than one or the other in isolation.

Peace of Mind grew slowly and organically over the years as I was immersed in an elementary school. This curriculum is the result of what I have learned works with real children. Our school is a kinder and more mindful place now and the children take these lessons to heart and take them with them into their lives after elementary school.

If you are a teacher, counselor, scout leader, youth group leader, or parent, you may be starting out small. That's great! I hope that this curriculum will give you some ideas and a foundation. I hope that you will take the opportunity to experiment and be creative and make your own version of *Peace of Mind*. This is what I have to offer. I hope it is helpful. Your community needs what you have to give.

Thank you for taking up this important work. The world needs mindful, peaceful people now more than ever.

In peace,

Linda

October 2015

Curriculum Overview

Peace [of Mind] Class teaches our children how to be part of a community that is kind, cooperative, intelligent, and emotionally healthy.

Janet Zwick, former teacher, Lafayette Elementary School

The **Peace of Mind** program includes innovative curricula that integrate mindfulness practice, social emotional learning, and conflict resolution for elementary school students. The goal of the **Peace of Mind** program is to help shift school cultures toward kindness and inclusion.

The **Peace of Mind Core Curriculum for Grades 3-5 (Peace of Mind)** helps students become emotionally, intellectually, and physically available to learn. The tools the curriculum teaches—mindfulness practices, conflict resolutions skills, and the habit of kindness—give students what they need to calm themselves and to focus in class. These tools also lead to less bullying and more external harmony and inclusion in the school community, allowing teachers to focus on teaching instead of discipline or conflict resolution.

Peace of Mind includes three **critical and interwoven** components marked by the following icons:

 Mindfulness

 Conflict Resolution

 Social and Emotional Learning (SEL)

Every lesson in this curriculum begins with mindfulness practice. Social Emotional Learning (SEL) lessons and conflict resolution practice are particularly effective because they are built upon this foundation.

Lesson themes include learning how to resolve conflicts peacefully, how to think before you speak, how to calm down when you are angry, what to do to help someone who is being bullied, and many others.

The curriculum uses storytelling, children's literature, sensory activities, role-playing, group discussion, and pair-sharing to bring these lessons to life. The key concepts are reinforced each year as children move from grade to grade, and adapted to be age-appropriate as the children grow.

Mindfulness Practice

Mindfulness is the practice of paying attention to our thoughts, our feelings, and what is happening around us, and putting some space between our reactions and our response.

Mindfulness practice can include quietly sitting to focus on breath awareness, walking mindfully, practicing mindful listening, learning a series of Mindful Movements, lessons in mindful eating, and much more. Mindfulness practice is becoming more popular in schools because research shows that creating deliberate moments of quiet and focus in a school day as part of a mindfulness-based social emotional learning program is likely to decrease anger, violence, and anxiety in a school (Weare, 2013).

Mindfulness practice in the classroom has also been shown to deliver many other benefits. Mindfulness training can help to enhance children's attention and focus (Zenner et al., 2014; Zoogman et al. 2015), improve self-control and emotion regulation (Metz et al., 2013), and improve overall social emotional competence including increased empathy, perspective-taking, and emotional control, and less peer-rated aggression (Schonert-Reichl et al., 2014; Schonert-Reichl & Lawlor, 2010).

> *Mindfulness can be understood as the foundation and basic precondition for education. Children need to learn to stop their mind wandering and regulate attention and emotions, deal with feelings of frustration, and to self-motivate. Mindfulness practice enhances the very qualities and goals of education in the 21st century (Zenner et al. 2014).*

Conflict Resolution

Peace of Mind grew out of an initial focus on teaching Conflict Resolution skills. As in many schools, students did not always seem to know how to work out conflicts, and often found themselves in fights at recess.

Building on the work of William Kreidler of Educators for Social Responsibility, **Peace of Mind** teaches the **Conflict CAT** as a way of remembering the three steps to working out a conflict.

C is for Calm Down   This is where students tap into their mindfulness practice.

A is for Apologize   Students can't be involved in an escalating conflict without doing or saying something for which they could apologize.

T is for Toolbox   The Conflict Toolbox is a list of eight ideas to help to work things out, such as sharing, taking turns, and compromising.

A parent at Lafayette Elementary School describes the impact of the conflict resolution portion of **Peace of Mind** with this powerful story:

> *I was a monitor during recess when I noticed two fourth graders get into a heated argument to the point of it getting physical… A third fourth grader who knew both of them interceded. He calmly talked to them both, using many of the tools Linda teaches— asking both what had happened, how they were feeling, and mentioning the "conflict escalator"… He helped the two boys resolve the issue and even got them to shake hands…*

> – Maria Petaros, Lafayette Elementary School parent

This deceptively simple and powerful model has given the children easy to remember steps to working out conflicts big and small.

Kindness Practice

Ultimately, the goal of **Peace of Mind** is to create a school culture of kindness. Creating a kinder, more positive school climate and dedicating class time for social emotional learning are two important and evidence-based approaches to bullying prevention (Bradshaw, 2015; O'Brennan & Bradshaw, 2013).

Through **Peace of Mind,** children learn how to practice mindfulness, to treat each other with kindness, to understand and manage their own feelings, and

to become active and engaged members of a positive and welcoming school community.

One foundation of building a culture of kindness is Kindness Pals. In this curriculum, every child is assigned a Kindness Pal each week. This is a very popular activity that achieves several goals. One is to remind the children to make kindness part of their daily lives. Doing kind things for their own "pal" spills over into their treatment of others. Pairing up the children also provides opportunities for them to get to know each other and to "find the good" in someone that they might not have gotten along with in the past or who they think they just don't like.

Teaching kindness can transform the culture of a school. Lafayette Elementary School Art teacher Laurie McLaughlin says:

> Students at Lafayette are demonstrating increasing skills in working as a team and supporting each other. There is a very positive and cooperative "vibe" this year at Lafayette, and I attribute that in part to Lafayette's unique Peace [of Mind] program.

Lafayette Elementary School Teacher Brad Jewett adds that:

> *The instances of bullying are down as children understand the scope of what bullying is. Linda's peace program has had a profound effect on our students.*

The lessons on kindness included in this curriculum offer many effective ways to engage students in practicing and reflecting on the importance of kindness inside and outside of the classroom.

Why these three components?

Mindfulness provides the critical foundation, the healthy soil, in which kindness and the peaceful resolution of conflicts can grow and bloom. Mindfulness helps children develop valuable internal skills: the ability to recognize their own feelings, and to increase their awareness of their surroundings and the feelings of others. Social Emotional Learning gives children tools to help them navigate relationships and conflicts. The combination of these internal and external skills is the magic behind **Peace of Mind**.

> *Ultimately, when taught and learned together, mindfulness and SEL have the potential to transform our communities and our world with the former cultivating the tendencies for compassion and ethical ways of living and the latter teaching the skills to make that happen.*
>
> Linda Lantieri, Senior Program Advisor for CASEL and Director of The Inner Resilience Program

How To Use
This Curriculum

Peace of Mind is different from other SEL programs in that mindfulness serves as the foundation for all of the conflict resolution and kindness and empathy lessons in the curriculum. Mindfulness practice increases children's attention and focus, enhancing the lesson for students and teacher alike.

This curriculum is comprised of 32 sequential weekly lessons. All of the lessons begin with mindfulness practice, the foundation for everything taught in this curriculum. After foundational mindfulness skills have been established and reviewed, the lessons build to include practice in conflict resolution, kindness, and empathy.

Lesson Planning

As you prepare to begin using **Peace of Mind**, please keep these key points in mind:

- The Mindfulness lessons and Conflict Resolution lessons that teach specific skills benefit from repetition, both during a year and from year to year. With repetition, students deepen and reinforce their ability to use the tools they are learning. Lessons that are particularly helpful to repeat are clearly marked. ⟫ REPEAT ME ⟫

- The lessons are designed to be taught in order, as each one builds on the ones that have come before.

- Some of these lessons can take as little as ten minutes; the longest could take 30 to 45 minutes in the older grades. The length of each lesson depends on the needs of the class and guidance of the teacher, and the engagement of the students in discussion.

Materials

The materials list for **Peace of Mind** is short:

- A bell or a chime of some sort;
- A means to show YouTube videos to your class;
- A Talking Object, such as a small stuffed animal or bean bag;
- Books and Videos. A list follows.

NOTE FROM LINDA: *I often use story books in my classes to help me to teach a lesson in a fun and memorable way. There is something about a well-told and beautifully illustrated storybook that helps an idea really stick in a child's mind. Over the years I often hear my students harken back to a story that I read to them two or three years ago. The children ask to hear these stories again and again and seem to get something new out of them at each developmental stage. I hope that these wonderful books will be available at your school or local library. If they aren't, please ask your librarian to order them. These are tried and true stories that have worked with all of my classes over the past twelve years. I hope you will enjoy these books as much as my students and I have.*

Books and Videos

This curriculum features the following books and videos. The books listed are age-appropriate storybooks. YouTube links for the videos are included in the relevant lessons and in the Resource section at the back of the curriculum.

Week 6	Steps and Stones by Gail Silver
Week 8	Enemy Pie by Derek Munson
Week 11	YouTube Video *Just Breathe*
Week 12	Rosie's Brain by Linda Ryden
Week 14	The Book of Awesome by Neil Pasricha
Week 16	"The Zax" by Dr. Seuss in The Sneetches and Other Stories
Week 19	Sorry by Trudy Ludwig
Week 28	*Don't Flip Yo Lid* by JusTme
Week 29	Say Something by Peggy Moss
Week 31	No Ordinary Apple by Sara Marlowe

Two Mainstays of *Peace of Mind*

Before beginning to teach **Peace of Mind**, please familiarize yourself with the two consistent features of every lesson: The Mindfulness Helper and Kindness Pals.

 The Mindfulness Helper

An important component of the mindfulness portion of the curriculum is a Mindfulness Helper. The Mindfulness Helper is a student who leads the class in Mindful Breathing to prepare for the lesson of the day. The Mindfulness Helper concept is introduced after basic ideas of mindful bodies, mindful listening, and mindful breathing have been established.

Where "Mindfulness Helper" is indicated you may follow these steps. The placement of the steps is indicated in each lesson that includes a Mindfulness Helper (MH).

- The teacher consults his or her alphabetical roll list and chooses a student to be the Mindfulness Helper for the day.

- The MH comes to the front of the class and sits next to the teacher on a chair.

- The MH chooses another student to turn off the classroom lights.

- The MH then says: "Let's get into our mindful bodies. Let's close our eyes. Let's take 3 deep breaths."

- At this point you can lead a mindfulness practice such as Heartfulness or do some mindful listening. If you are just doing a brief mindful moment, move on to the next step.

- The MH rings the bell when the mindful breathing is complete.

- The MH asks a classmate to turn on the lights.

- The teacher then asks the MH to return to his or her seat.

The teacher may need to help younger students to remember what to say at the beginning of the year. Repeating the same words each class is important to help students develop a routine to help them begin to practice on their own.

 Kindness Pals

Kindness Pals is a very popular activity that achieves several goals:

- To remind the children to make kindness part of their daily lives. Doing kind things for their Kindness Pals spills over into their treatment of others.

- To develop the habit of treating people with kindness through regular practice.

- To give children opportunities to get to know each other and to "find the good" in others whom they might not have gotten along with in the past or whom they think they just don't like.

Here is how it works:

- Each week you assign each student one Kindness Pal. You can pair up the children in advance using the Kindness Pals template (see the Resource Section) or you can write the children's names on index cards and have them pull a name out of a hat. If you have children in your class with special needs, pair them up with children likely to be kind to them rather than leaving it to chance.

- When children receive the names of their Pals, emphasize that both pals must say "Okay." This is very important. This lets the teacher know that they have heard their assignment and that they know who their Kindness Pals are.

- Please let the class know that this is not a time for them to let the teacher or the class know how they feel about having that Kindness Pal. This avoids hurt feelings and also offers multiple chances to remind the children that they have the power to be kind and the power to hurt people's feelings. It all depends on their choices. This is a powerful lesson.

- Explain to the students that they will each receive one Kindness Pal each week. It is their job to do nice things for their assigned Kindness Pals for the whole week. Some examples of kind behavior might be to get a pal's snack, stack her chair, or play together at recess.

- The following week, allow children to talk about what they did for their Pal, allowing about 5 minutes for this sharing. You may need to limit the time because it is too much, or perhaps to use a counter of some sort to keep track and motivate a class that isn't doing such a great job.

- Then, assign new Pals for the week ahead.

If you are a classroom teacher you can use Kindness Pals as partners, field trip buddies, and so on. You may allow time for kids to make cards or other things for their Kindness Pal. Kids love it!

Self-Preparation

All that's left is to prepare yourself.

Daniel Rechtschaffen in his book, The Way of Mindful Education, tells this story:

A mother once brought her son to Mahatma Gandhi, asking him if he could please give the boy a lecture on how bad it was to eat too many sweets.

Gandhi replied that she should return in two weeks. When the weeks passed she brought her son back and Gandhi gave an articulate speech about how unhealthy sweets were to the body and the mind. The mother was appreciative, but confused. 'Why didn't you just tell him this two weeks ago?' she asked. 'Well at that time I was eating too many sweets myself.' Gandhi replied.

It is so important to establish your own mindfulness practice before you attempt to teach it to your students. Just as you would never try to teach Spanish before you learned the language yourself, it is important to begin your own mindfulness practice before bringing these simple but transformative skills to your students.

There are so many great resources to help you get started. The App called Headspace is a wonderful, secular, and simple step-by-step mindfulness program. There are also many free resources on line. You don't have to be an expert in mindfulness but it is important to join your students on the journey.

I think mindful breathing and kindness pals are important. Mindful breathing helps me calm down when I have a lot on my mind and kindness pals helps me make new friends.

Peace of Mind Student at Lafayette Elementary School, Washington D.C.

Even if I come to Peace class sad or not feeling well or just in a bad mood, I always become very calm and happy by the end…everything about Peace class is wonderful. I love it!!

Lessons

Peace of Mind for Third to Fifth Grade

Teaching Mindfulness to older elementary students is very rewarding. Unlike the younger kids, they are often able to sit for longer periods of time and seem to really understand how mindfulness skills are helpful to them in their daily lives. Children around this age are very interested in learning about themselves and are open to learning how to become more aware of what is happening in their minds and in their hearts.

Mindfulness lessons for this age group focus primarily on breathing and understanding how our own minds work. Mindfulness practice can help children to recognize when they are getting angry and to assist them in staying calm. In a calm state, children can use the skills taught in the conflict resolution lessons to work out conflicts peacefully, instead of avoiding them or losing control.

Most kids are very open to learning about mindfulness. But, if you find that you have to do a little convincing, it can be very helpful to relate mindfulness to sports. Many sports teams and sports stars such as the Seattle Seahawks, Kobe Bryant, and Lebron James practice mindfulness regularly to enhance their performance. Talking about how mindfulness practice can help us play better by helping us focus, control our temper, be more of a team player, connect our minds and bodies, and calming our nerves can be very influential to student athletes. This can also be true of music, dance, and just about anything else that your students are interested in. Finding the relevance can be important, especially for the older elementary students.

The Social and Emotional Learning (SEL) Lessons in this section focus on the power of words to help or hurt. It is important for children to start to understand how powerful their words can be, and how it is impossible to take our words back once they are out of our mouths. Many of these lessons are designed to help children start to be more mindful of what they say to others and to take a moment to consider how their words will make other people feel before speaking.

Kindness Pals, described in detail in the previous "How To Use This Curriculum" chapter, is an important component of all lessons.

NOTE FROM LINDA: *In this curriculum, I have grouped third through fifth grades together. In reality, there are some significant developmental differences within those years. In my years of teaching, I have found that third graders can sometimes be more like rising fourth graders and sometimes more like recent second graders. If you feel your third graders are on the young side, you might consider using lessons included in the first book in this series, Core Curriculum for Grades 1-2, and mixing in some of the lessons from this book. In short, I trust you to use your professional judgment to choose the lessons to fit the needs of the children you are trying to reach.*

Managing Expectations

Keep your expectations reasonable. Some kids have a much easier time sitting quietly than others. Sometimes the kid who is sitting with his eyes wide open, legs jiggling, and fiddling with a pencil—but not talking—during mindfulness practice is doing his very best and is benefiting greatly from the effort. That's okay. The exercises in this curriculum are for the benefit of the children and, as long as it is not preventing other children from practicing, a little wiggling around is okay.

Goals for Third, Fourth and Fifth Grade

Upon completion of this curriculum, 3rd, 4th and 5th graders
will be able to:

- Use breathing to help manage challenging emotions, like anger or frustration.

- Be more aware of their thoughts and feelings, especially challenging feelings such as worry and anxiety.

- Use Mindfulness to calm themselves and focus their attention.

- Understand that their thoughts do not have to control their actions.

- Understand brain function as it relates to being able to calm oneself.

- Practice the habit of being kind.

- Understand and use the Conflict Resolution Tool Kit to resolve conflicts with friends and siblings at school and at home.

Week 1
Introduction to Mindfulness

(handwritten in top right margin: Mindful Bodies Breathing)

OBJECTIVES: Introduce the concept of mindfulness and create the foundation for mindfulness practice.

Introduce Kindness Pals.

PREPARE: A bell or chime

Your Kindness Pals list and Talking Object

 1. Introduce the lesson by saying:

Today we are going to start learning about something new together. It's called mindfulness.

Mindfulness is fun because anyone can do it, you can do it anywhere, and you have everything you need to do it right in your own body. You have probably tried it already and didn't even know it.

Mindfulness is about noticing things. Sometimes we'll notice things by listening or seeing or even by sitting quietly with our eyes closed. Sometimes we'll be moving, and sometimes we'll be eating!

Are you ready to start?

The first thing we are going to do is listen.

I'd like you to close or cover your eyes and I'm going to set a timer for thirty seconds. During that time I want you to count inside your mind, not out loud, how many different sounds you hear.

Try not to make any sounds yourself, just sit really still and count the sounds you hear. You might have to listen really hard to hear things. Ready? Close your eyes. Okay let's start listening now…

Wait about thirty seconds or longer if they seem to have an easy time staying still. You might subtly add some sounds (chair squeaking, footsteps, keys softly jingling, etc.) if the room is really quiet.

Say: *Now let's open our eyes.*

2. Discuss

Leave plenty of time for sharing. You might use these kinds of questions to frame a discussion:

- Who would like to tell us about a sound that you heard?
- How did you know it was a door squeaking if you couldn't see the door?

Try to hear from everyone, even if they are sharing about a sound that had already been mentioned.

If you are short on time, have them share with an elbow partner instead.

3. Beyond the classroom

Conclude this portion of the lesson by encouraging students to use mindful listening at home.

Say:

Isn't it interesting how many different sounds we could hear?

All of these sounds were all around us and yet we weren't paying attention to them.

This is something you can try anytime—when you are at home, or in the car, or outside on the playground. Just stop and take a moment to do some mindful listening.

4. Introduce Mindful Bodies.

Say: *We are going to practice being mindful every time we meet. Whenever we do our mindfulness we are going to get into a special position called a Mindful Body.*

Guide the children into their Mindful Bodies.

If you have the space and time, it is wonderful to have everyone sitting on the floor on a rug, carpet squares, or little cushions.

If the students are at their desks, ask them to turn their chairs toward the front of the room or move a bit away from their desks in order to reduce distractions.

Ask them to sit up nice and straight, feet on the floor if they reach, and put their hands in their laps.

5. Practice getting into Mindful Bodies a few times.

Ask the children to feel the difference between the way we normally sit and the way we sit when we are ready to be mindful.

Talk about what it means to be "ready" and how this relates to other activities they may participate in.

Ask the students to describe the "ready position" for the batter in a baseball game, for a soccer goalie, or for a tennis player waiting to return a serve.

Ask: How do children on the playground get into "ready position" before a race or before beginning to jump rope?

Ask: How does a musician or a dancer get his or her body into position so that she or he is ready to play or perform?

Then you might say:

In the "ready position," you have noticed that your feet might be still, your body might be in one particular position that's best for the activity you are about to start, and your mind is focused and alert. All of these are to help you do the best you can do in the sport or game or performance ahead. The same is true for mindfulness practice. We get into our Mindful Bodies so that we are in the best possible ready position to be able to use our mindfulness practice to calm ourselves and improve our focus and attention.

6. Introduce a Mindful Listening activity.

Ask students to get into their Mindful Bodies.

Ask the students to close their eyes.

Ask them to listen to the bell and raise their hands when they can no longer hear the sound.

♡ Kindness Pals

Introduce Kindness Pals as follows:

Now we are going to start something called Kindness Pals. Every time we meet, I am going to give you a Kindness Pal. It will be a different person in your class each time. I'm going to ask you to do something kind for this person between now and the next time we meet. It can be something small like stacking their chair or something bigger like drawing them a picture, making them a card, or playing with them at recess. You can even do more than one thing.

Can you think of other kind things you could do for your Kindness Pal?

Give them time to share.

I have one very important rule about Kindness Pals. Since the whole point of Kindness Pals is to help us practice being kind, I want to make sure that we start out with kindness. So when I tell you who your Kindness Pal is going to be, I want you to say "okay" in a friendly way. Let's try that all together: "Okay!"

When I tell you who your Kindness Pal is, you might feel really happy and excited. Maybe your Kindness Pal is already your really good friend, and it will be really easy to be kind to them.

But sometimes when I tell you who your Kindness Pal is, you might feel differently. You might feel a little nervous or shy. And that's fine. Any way that you feel is fine. But in that moment I want you to try really hard to be kind to your Pal and say a nice, friendly "Okay!" That way your Pal will know that you are ready to show them some kindness.

You don't have to become friends with your Pal (although you might), and you don't even have to like your Pal. All I'm asking you to do is to find some way to be kind to them this week.

When we meet next time, I'm going to ask you to try to remember something that you did for your Kindness Pal and share it with the class. Are you ready to find out who your Kindness Pal is?

Read through the list, saying, for example, "Rosie and Henry are Kindness Pals."

Wait for the "Okay" before moving on.

Say: *Now that you know who your Kindness Pal is, we're going to find out a little more about them. Who can think of a question that we could ask our Kindness Pal?*

Listen to students' suggestions. They might suggest asking about their favorite color or favorite food or sport.

Choose three questions.

Ask the students to sit with their Kindness Pals and have a little chat.

Share. If you have time, you can come back together as a group and ask them to share something that they learned about their Kindness Pals. This exercise is a great way to practice Mindful Listening and help them to develop an interest in others.

Say: *Okay, so now we've gotten to know our Kindness Pal a little better. I can't wait until next time when we get to hear about the kind things you did for your Pal. Have fun!*

Closing words: *Thanks for a great class, everyone. Let's have a nice quiet moment with the bell. You can close your eyes or leave them open but let's sit quietly and listen to the bell. If you want to, you can think about your new Kindness Pal and imagine yourself doing something kind for them.*

Ring the bell or chime.

Week 2
Mindful Breathing

OBJECTIVES: Introduce the foundation mindfulness exercise.
Practice kindness.

PREPARE: A bell or chime
Your Kindness Pals list and Talking Object

1. Introduce mindful breathing to the class.

You might say:

Today we are going to talk about breathing. Breathing is something you do all day and night, but you hardly ever think about it. When are some times that you might be more aware or mindful of your breath?

Allow children to answer. Their responses will likely be along the lines of: when you are "out of breath" after a big run, when you are angry and breathing hard, and so on.

2. Lead the class in a mindful breathing exercise. You might say:

Today we are going to be mindful of our breathing. First, let's get into our mindful bodies. Let's keep our eyes open for now.

Put one hand on your belly and see what you notice. Does your belly go in and out when you breathe? Keep your hand there and notice what that feels like for a few breaths. Now move your hand to your chest. What do you notice here?

Now make your hand like a little cup under your nose. Can you feel the breath going in and out? Do you notice that the breath feels a little bit cooler going in and a little bit warmer going out?"

Now I'd like you to choose one of the three places where we could feel our breath—in the belly, the chest, under the nose—and choose the place where you could feel your breath the most. Now, let's all close or cover our eyes. We are going to try to focus our minds on our breath for a few seconds. See if you notice if all of your breaths feel the same or if some are different.

Ask students to open their eyes and share what they noticed about their breath.

 Kindness Pals

Say: *Last time we met I gave you Kindness Pals and asked you to do something kind for them. Did anybody remember to do something for their Pal?*

Who would like to share what you did?

I'm going to pass the talking object to someone who is ready to share. When you are holding the talking object it is your turn to share. If you are not holding the talking object it is your turn to listen.

Pass the object to someone. When the student is finished speaking, pass it to his or her Kindness Pal who can either share what he did, or simply say "Thank you" to his Pal. This little practice helps the children to develop a sense of gratitude for little kindnesses.

Assign new Kindness Pals after they are finished sharing. See the instructions in the "How To Use This Curriculum" section.

If you have time, you can give them time for a Kindness pal chat like they had in Lesson 1.

Closing words: *Our time is up for today. Thank you for a great class, everyone.*

Let's have a nice quiet moment for the bell. If you want to, you can close your eyes, picture your new Kindness Pal, and imagine yourself doing something kind for him or her this week.

Ring the bell.

Week 3
Mindful Breathing 2

OBJECTIVES: Practice a fundamental skill of Mindfulness.

Practice kindness.

PREPARE: A bell or chime

 1. Introduce Lesson

You might say:

Today we are going to continue practicing Mindful breathing. Last time we focused on our breath. Today we are going to do that again.

Put your hands on your belly and take a few breaths.

Did you notice that your breath has two parts? The breath goes in and the breath goes out. Today we are going to focus on our breath.

But first, let's get set up to practice.

2. Introduce Mindfulness Helper

Say: *Today I am going to ask someone to come up and help me lead the mindfulness practice. Every class I'll choose a different person to be the Mindfulness Helper.*

Consult your alphabetical roll list, and choose the first student to be the Mindfulness Helper for the day.

Invite today's Mindfulness Helper (MH) to come to the front of the class to sit next to you on a chair.

Prompt the MH to choose another student to turn off the classroom lights.

Prompt the MH to say slowly:

- Let's get into our mindful bodies. Pause
- Let's close our eyes. Pause
- Let's take 3 deep breaths. Pause

3. Mindful Breathing

Say: *Let your breath settle back into its natural rhythm. You don't have to change it at all.*

While you are breathing, place your hand on your belly and feel the little movement that happens when your breath goes in and out.

Now move your hand to your chest and see what you feel there when your breath goes in and out. Notice where you felt your breath the most and keep your hand there, either on your belly or your chest.

Now we're going to count ten breaths. You can count them any way you want to. You can count one in-breath, or inhale, and one out-breath, or exhale, as one whole breath. Or you can count each inhale and exhale as one breath. It doesn't matter how you count them. Try to keep your mind focused on counting your breaths.

As soon as you notice that your mind has wandered away, try to bring it back to your counting, starting again at one. Try not to count higher than ten. Once you get to ten, start over at one.

Okay, let's try it. Remember, this is just for fun. Don't worry if your mind wanders. Just try to bring it back when you notice it has wandered. Let's start now.

You can give them a minute or more to try this, whatever seems appropriate.

Okay, now you can stop focusing on your counting, and let your mind be free to think or not think, whatever your mind wants to do.

Wait about 15 seconds.

Now let's take one more deep breath in and out. In a moment you will hear the sound of the bell and that will mean that it is time to open your eyes.

Ask the MH to ring the bell when the mindful breathing is complete.

Ask the MH to choose a classmate to turn the lights on.

Ask the MH to return to his or her seat.

4. Reflection

Ask:

- What was that like for you?
- Was it hard to keep your mind focused on your breath?
- Did counting help you to focus?

Try to practice this a couple of times this week and see if it gets any easier.

 Kindness Pals

Say: *Last time we met I gave you Kindness Pals and asked you to do something kind for them. Did anybody remember to do something for their Pal?*

Who would like to share what you did?

I'm going to pass the talking object to someone who is ready to share. When you are holding the talking object it is your turn to share. If you are not holding the talking object it is your turn to listen.

Pass the object to someone. When the student is finished speaking, pass it to his or her Kindness Pal who can either share what he did, or simply say "Thank you" to his Pal. This little practice helps the children to develop a sense of gratitude for little kindnesses.

Assign new Kindness Pals after they are finished sharing. See the instructions in the "How To Use This Curriculum" section.

If you have time, you can give them time for a Kindness pal chat like they had in Lesson 1.

Closing words: *Our time is up for today. Thank you for a great class, everyone.*

Let's have a nice quiet moment for the bell. If you want to, you can close your eyes, picture your new Kindness Pal, and imagine yourself doing something kind for him or her this week.

Ring the bell.

Week 4
Mindfulness of Thoughts

OBJECTIVES:	Introduce the foundational mindfulness skill of focusing on the breath.
	Practice kindness.
PREPARE:	A bell or chime
	Review the rules of the "Thoughts" Game
	Your Kindness Pals list and Talking Object

 1. Introduce the Lesson

Ask: *When I ask you to close your eyes and focus your mind on a sound or on your breath, what happens?*

Stop and let them share.

Yes, one thing we all notice is that our minds wander. The good news is that this is perfectly normal. It happens to everyone.

The difference is that when your mind wanders when you are in math class you might not notice it until the teacher calls on you and you suddenly realize you have no idea what is going on. That's not a great feeling.

In Mindfulness, we are trying to notice that moment when our minds wander and see where our minds go. Then we can decide if we want to redirect our minds. That's part of the fun.

Tell *the students that you are going to be playing a game called "Thoughts."*

Describe *the game like this:*

I'm going to ask you to close your eyes and focus on counting your breath just the way we did in the last lesson. Once we start counting our breaths, I want you to try to pay attention to your mind.

As soon as you notice that your mind has wandered, that a thought or a feeling has come into your mind, just point your finger.

Then see if you can bring your mind back to focusing on counting your breaths. Keep doing this until I ask you to stop. Let's try it.

2. Introduce Mindfulness Helper

Invite today's Mindfulness Helper (MH) to come to the front of the class to sit next to you on a chair.

Prompt the MH to choose another student to turn off the classroom lights.

Prompt the MH to say: "Let's get into our mindful bodies. Let's close our eyes. Let's take 3 deep breaths."

3. Play "Thoughts" as described above.

Say: *Now let your breath settle back into its natural rhythm. Just breathe. Put your hand on your belly to help you to focus on your breath.*

When you are ready, start to count your breaths. Every time you notice that your mind has wandered away from your breath, when a thought has popped into your mind, just point your finger and try to gently bring your mind back to your breath. You might have to do this over and over. That's perfectly fine.

Wait about a minute or so and then say: *Now you can just let your mind be free to think or not think.*

After a moment say: *Now let's take a nice deep breath and listen for the sound of the bell. When you hear the bell it will be time to open your eyes.*

Ask the MH to ring the bell when the "Thoughts" Exercise is complete.

Ask the MH to choose a classmate to turn the lights on.

Ask the MH to return to his or her seat.

4. Reflect

After the game is over ask:

- Did you notice that you were pointing your finger a lot today?

- What did it feel like to pay attention to those thoughts as they came in?
- What kinds of thoughts did you notice today?

 Kindness Pals

Do the Kindness Pal activity as before.

Closing words: *Okay our time is up for today. Thank you for a great class, everyone.*

Let's have a nice quiet moment for the bell. If you want to, you can close your eyes, picture your new Kindness Pal, and imagine yourself doing something kind for them this week.

Ring the bell.

Week 5
Where Are Your Thoughts?

OBJECTIVES: Notice if your thoughts are mostly about the past or the future and help students stay in the present moment.

Practice kindness.

PREPARE: A bell or chime

Your Kindness Pals list and Talking Object

 1. Introduce the Lesson

You might say:

The last time we met we practiced noticing our thoughts. We pointed our fingers every time a thought came into our minds.

Today we are going to be trying to notice if our thoughts are about the past, the present, or the future.

If I am thinking about my basketball game tomorrow my thoughts are in the.... **(future)**.

If I am thinking about an argument I had with my little brother last night, my thoughts are in the.... **(past)**.

If you are focusing on listening to me right now, your thoughts are in the.... **(present)**.

So today, after we get set up by the Mindfulness Helper, we are going to try to count our breaths.

Only this time, every time you notice that your mind has wandered (and you know it will!) I want you to try to notice if it is a thought about the past, the present, or the future.

Once you've labeled that thought, see if you can bring your mind back to counting your breaths. **You might want to demonstrate this for them.**

2. Mindfulness Helper

Invite today's Mindfulness Helper (MH) to come to the front of the class and sit next to you on a chair.

Prompt the MH to choose another student to turn off the classroom lights.

Prompt the MH to say: "Let's get into our mindful bodies. Let's close our eyes. Let's take 3 deep breaths."

3. Exercise: Lead the class through Past-Present-Future as described above.

Ask the MH to ring the bell when the "Thoughts" Exercise is complete.

Ask the MH to choose a classmate to turn the lights on.

Ask the MH to return to his or her seat.

4. Discuss and Reflect

After the exercise is over say:

- Raise your hand if most of your thoughts were about the past.
- Raise your hand if most of your thoughts were in the present.
- Raise your hand if most of your thoughts were in the future.
- Raise your hand if you had a mixture.

Ask some of the children to share one of the thoughts they noticed and then let other children guess if the thought was in the past, present, or future. This isn't always easy and there can be more than one right answer.

Ask:

- Why do you think it might be good to keep your mind focused on the present, on this moment?
- If your mind is always focused on what has already happened, or what hasn't happened yet, or what might never happen, what do you think you might be missing?

Discuss

- When we try to notice where our thoughts are going, we can try to redirect them to where we want them to be. If you tend to worry a lot, your thoughts are mostly in the…. (future).
- Worrying doesn't help make things better and it doesn't stop bad things from happening. But it does keep you from enjoying the good stuff.
- If you notice that your thoughts are often in the future, see if you can try to focus your mind on something right here in the present moment. Try to notice what is good in this moment.

 Kindness Pals

Do the Kindness Pal activity as before.

Closing words: *Okay our time is up for today. Thank you for a great class, everyone.*

Let's have a nice quiet moment for the bell. If you want to, you can close your eyes, picture your new Kindness Pal, and imagine yourself doing something kind for them this week.

Ring the bell.

Week 6
Using Mindfulness to Take Care of Anger

OBJECTIVES: Read the story to illustrate the concept of using
                mindful breathing to handle strong emotions.

                Practice kindness.

PREPARE: A bell or chime

                The Hoberman sphere

                Steps and Stones by Gail Silver

                Your Kindness Pal list and Talking Object

 Mindfulness Practice

Invite today's Mindfulness Helper (MH) to come to the front of the class
to sit next to you on a chair.

Prompt the MH to choose another student to turn off the classroom lights.

Prompt the MH to say: "Let's get into our mindful bodies. Let's close our
eyes. Let's take 3 deep breaths."

Say: *Now let your breath settle back into its natural rhythm. Just breathe in and
out. Put a hand on your tummy and see if you can make the rest of your body so
still that they only thing that you feel moving is your breath.*

*Now let's begin to count your breaths like we did in the last couple of lessons.
You can raise your finger when you notice that your mind has wandered away
from your breathing. Remember not to worry if your mind wanders away over
and over. The important thing is to notice what is happening in your mind.*

Wait a minute or two.

Say: *In a moment you will hear the sound of the bell (****or chime or whatever
you are using****). When you hear that sound, it will be time to open your eyes.*

Ask the MH to ring the bell when the mindful breathing is complete.

Ask the MH to choose a classmate to turn the lights back on.

Ask the MH to return to his or her seat.

1. Introduce the Lesson

Say: *Today we are going to read a book about a boy who gets angry at school. Is getting angry at school harder than getting angry at home? What is different?*

2. Read <u>Steps and Stones</u>

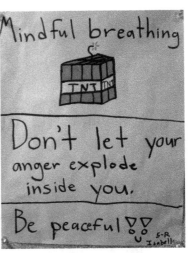

This is a story about a boy who gets angry at school. He learns to take care of his anger by walking mindfully and counting his steps.

3. Discuss

Ask:

- Why is Anh angry?
- What did Anh's anger look like?
- Anh's anger says that he's not sure if anger is allowed in school. Is it?

Say:

It might seem like anger isn't allowed in school, but it is important to remember that all of our feelings are always allowed. But sometimes we are not in a place where we can express them the way we might want to. Like at school. This is why our mindful breathing can be so helpful.

Ask:

- What would have happened if Anh had listened to his anger and thrown the ball at Charlie?
- What did Anh do instead?
- How did the slow walk and the breathing help him?
- What happened to his anger?

Teach Take Five Breathing

Take Five is a nice way to help children calm themselves down when they are upset or need a break. Here's a sample script to use to introduce the concept.

You might say:

Today we're going to learn another way of using our mindful breathing. Has anyone ever heard someone say "Take Five?"

Take Five means to take a break—usually they mean a five-minute break. We are going to use Take Five in a different way. Hold up your hand like you are going to give someone a high five with your palm facing out and your fingers spread wide.

Now take the index finger of your other hand and trace the outline of your hand. What does it feel like when your finger runs between your fingers? Maybe it's a little tickly?

We're going to do this again, but this time we are going to breathe in when we are tracing up and breathe out when we are tracing down. Starting with your index finger down by your wrist on the outside of your thumb as you trace up your thumb, slowly breathe in, and as your trace down the inside of your thumb slowly breathe out.

Repeat this motion with all of your fingers until you are back down at your wrist on the outside of your pinky finger. At this point you will have taken five deep breaths.

Take Five is a great way to help you calm down any time you feel angry or scared or nervous or worried or stressed out or just need a break. See if you can try it a few times this week.

 Kindness Pals

Do the Kindness Pals activity as before.

Closing words: *Okay our time is up for today. Thank you for a great class, everyone. Let's have a nice quiet moment for the bell. If you want to, you can close your eyes, picture your new Kindness Pal, and imagine yourself doing something kind for them this week.*

Ring the bell.

Week 7
Keeping Your Focus

OBJECTIVES: Practice keeping your focus when surrounded by annoying sounds.

Practice kindness.

PREPARE: A bell or chime

Gather noisemakers, such as scissors, a wind-up toy, a jar of pencils, a squeaky chair, etc. Use whatever you have around.

Your Kindness Pals list and Talking Object

1. Introduce Lesson

You might say:

Today I am going to challenge you. After the Mindfulness Helper gets us set up, I am going to ask you to focus your mind on counting your breaths.

While you are doing that I'm going to be really annoying.

I'm going to be making some sounds and trying to distract you. Your job is to keep your eyes closed, even if you are really curious, and keep your mind focused on counting your breaths.

Anytime you get distracted you can go back and start counting at one. I will show you everything I used to make the sounds when we are done so don't be tempted to peek. Ready?

2. Mindfulness Helper

Invite today's Mindfulness Helper (MH) to come to the front of the class to sit next to you on a chair.

Prompt the MH to choose another student to turn off the classroom lights.

Prompt the MH to say: "Let's get into our mindful bodies. Let's close our eyes. Let's take 3 deep breaths."

Say: *Now I'd like you to try to start counting your breaths. As I said before I am going to try to distract you. I might make noises or do other things to take your focus off of your breath. Try really hard to keep your focus on counting your breaths. and don't open your eyes to peek. We'll share what happened when we are finished.*

3. Keep Your Focus Exercise

Distract the class. After the children are set up and have begun their mindful breathing practice, you are going to try to distract them by being really annoying.

Walk around the room and make random noises. You might even tap someone on the top of the head or whisper someone's name.

Their job is to keep their eyes closed and try to keep focusing on counting their breaths.

Say: *Now take a deep breath, and listen for the sound of the bell. When you hear that sound it will be time to open your eyes.*

Ask the MH to ring the bell.

Ask the MH to choose a classmate to turn the lights on.

Ask the MH to return to his or her seat

4. Discuss and Reflect

After the exercise, **ask**:

- Can you guess what I was using to make the sounds?
- What did you hear?
- Was it hard or easy to keep your focus?

 Kindness Pals

Do the Kindness Pal activity as before.

Closing words: *Okay our time is up for today. Thank you for a great class, everyone.*

Let's have a nice quiet moment for the bell. If you want to, you can close your eyes, picture your new Kindness Pal, and imagine yourself doing something kind for them this week.

Ring the bell.

Week 8
Enemy Pie

OBJECTIVES: Learn the importance of getting to know people and not judging them.

PREPARE: A bell or chime

<u>Enemy Pie</u> by Derek Munson

Your Kindness Pals list and Talking Object

 Mindfulness Practice

Invite today's Mindfulness Helper (MH) to come to the front of the class to sit next to you on a chair.

Prompt the MH to choose another student to turn off the classroom lights.

Prompt the MH to say: "Let's get into our mindful bodies. Let's close our eyes. Let's take 3 deep breaths."

Say: *Now let your breath settle back into its natural rhythm. Just breathe in and out. Put a hand on your tummy and see if you can make the rest of your body so still that they only thing that you feel moving is your breath.*

Now let's begin to count your breaths like we did in the last couple of lessons. You can raise your finger when you notice that your mind has wandered away from your breathing. Remember not to worry if your mind wanders away over and over. The important thing is to notice what is happening in your mind.

Wait a minute or two.

Say: *In a moment you will hear the sound of the bell* (**or chime or whatever you are using**). *When you hear that sound, it will be time to open your eyes.*

Ask the MH to ring the bell when the mindful breathing is complete.

Ask the MH to choose a classmate to turn the lights back on.

Ask the MH to return to his or her seat.

1. Read <u>Enemy Pie</u>

Enemy Pie is a hilarious story about a father helping his son learn a lesson. The boy has an enemy and his father says that he has a sure-fire way to get rid of enemies called Enemy Pie. It turns out that the real secret is that the boy has to spend an entire day with his enemy. By the end of the day, the two boys are friends.

2. Discussion

You might use these questions to guide the discussion of the story:

- Why was the boy telling the story mad at his enemy?
- Did he know him well at the beginning of the story?
- Did the enemy pie work?
- Was his father tricking him?
- What is the real secret of enemy pie?

3. Commonalities Game

Direct everyone to sit next to his or her Kindness Pal or a partner.

Give them three minutes to come up with all of the things that they have in common. Don't have them write them down. This will encourage mindful listening instead of writing.

Ask everyone to share what he or she had in common with their partners.

Ask them to share if there were any surprises.

 Kindness Pals

Do the Kindness Pal activity as before.

Closing words: *Okay our time is up for today. Thank you for a great class, everyone.*

Let's have a nice quiet moment for the bell. If you want to, you can close your eyes, picture your new Kindness Pal, and imagine yourself doing something kind for them this week.

Ring the bell.

Week 9
Body Scan

OBJECTIVES:	Learn that we can be aware of what is happening in our bodies and begin to relate those physical feelings to our emotions.
	Practice kindness.
PREPARE:	A bell or chime
	Your Kindness Pals list and Talking Object

1. Introduce a New Mindfulness Exercise

Use this script:

Let's get into our Mindful Bodies. I'm going to clap my hands and I want you to watch how I do it.

Put your arms out in front of you with your palms facing each other. Clap your hands together hard and leave your hands about a foot apart. You will notice an intense tingling feeling.

Now, I want you to you to close your eyes or look down into your lap if you don't feel comfortable closing your eyes, and put your arms out in front of you like I did. When I say 'Go' we are all going to clap our hands. Make sure that you don't talk, but just quietly notice what you feel. Go.

Give them a moment to notice the feelings.

Open your eyes or look up when you can't feel that tingling anymore.

Discuss what that felt like.

2. Mindfulness Helper

Say: *Today we are going to take a little trip around our bodies with our minds.*

Invite today's Mindfulness Helper (MH) to come to the front of the class to sit next to you on a chair.

Prompt the MH to choose another student to turn off the classroom lights.

Prompt the MH to say: "Let's get into our mindful bodies. Let's close our eyes. Let's take 3 deep breaths."

Say: *Now listen for the sound of the bell. When you hear that sound it will be time to open your eyes.*

Ask the MH to ring the bell.

Ask the MH to choose a classmate to turn the lights on.

Ask the MH to return to his or her seat.

3. Body Scan

Say: *Let's get into our Mindful Bodies again and close or cover our eyes. I want you to start by thinking about the top of your head. Imagine that you can touch the top of your head, not with your hand, but with your mind. It's like you're touching the top of your head from the inside. Can you feel anything when you focus your mind on the top of your head?* **Pause**.

Now let's travel down into our faces. Try to feel your forehead – does it feel tight and scrunched? What does it feel like if you try to make it feel more relaxed and smooth? Notice your mouth – is it hanging loose and down? Notice what it feels like if you smile a little bit. **Pause**.

Try to notice your ears – can you feel your ears with your mind? Let's travel down to your neck and shoulders. Notice if your shoulders are tight and high. What does it feel like if you soften and lower your shoulders a bit? **Pause.**

Let the attention travel down your right arm all the way down to your fingers. Do you remember how your hands felt after you clapped them together? Does your hand feel different now? What do you notice?

Let your attention travel down your other arm to your other hand? What do you notice there? Now let your mind travel down your back. Is your back nice and straight or are you hunched over? Notice what it feels like to have a nice, straight back.

Notice the weight of your body on the chair or on the rug or cushion. Let your mind travel down your legs. Do your legs feel the same or different from each other? Try to pay attention to each one of your toes. Give them a little wiggle. Now bring your attention back up to the top of your head and try to sweep down through your whole body. Which foot is warmer?

4. Reflect and Discuss

Ask the students to open their eyes. Use these questions to guide a discussion.

- What did it feel like to travel through your body?
- What did you notice?
- Are you used to paying attention to your body?
- Would it be helpful to pay more attention to your body?
- What about when you are playing a sport?

 Kindness Pals

Do the Kindness Pal activity as before.

Closing words: *Okay our time is up for today. Thank you for a great class, everyone.*

Let's have a nice quiet moment for the bell. If you want to, you can close your eyes, picture your new Kindness Pal, and imagine yourself doing something kind for them this week.

Ring the bell.

Week 10
Deep Belly Breathing

OBJECTIVES: Learn deep belly breathing to help manage strong emotions.

Practice kindness.

PREPARE: A bell or chime

Your Kindness Pals list and Talking Object

 Mindfulness Practice

Invite today's Mindfulness Helper (MH) to come to the front of the class to sit next to you on a chair.

Prompt the MH to choose another student to turn off the classroom lights.

Prompt the MH to say: "Let's get into our mindful bodies. Let's close our eyes. Let's take 3 deep breaths."

Say: *Let your breath settle back into its natural rhythm. You don't have to change it at all.*

While you are breathing, place your hand on your belly and feel the little movement that happens when your breath goes in and out.

Now move your hand to your chest and see what you feel there when your breath goes in and out. Try to notice where you felt your breath the most and keep your hand there, either on your belly or your chest.

Now we're going to count ten breaths. You can count them any way you want to. You can count one in-breath, or inhale, and one out-breath, or exhale, as one whole breath. Or you can count each inhale and exhale. It doesn't matter how you count them. Try to keep your mind focused on counting your breaths.

As soon as you notice that your mind has wandered away, try to bring it back to your counting starting again at one. Try not to count higher than ten. Once you get to ten, start over at one.

| http://www.teachpeaceofmind.com

Okay, let's try it. Remember, this is just for fun. Don't worry if your mind wanders. Just try to bring it back when you notice it has wandered. Let's start now.

You can give them a minute or more to try this, whatever seems appropriate.

Okay, now you can stop focusing on your counting and let your mind be free to think or not think, whatever your mind wants to do.

Wait about 15 seconds.

Now let's take one more deep breath in and out. In a moment you will hear the sound of the bell and that will mean that it is time to open your eyes.

Ask the MH to ring the bell when the mindful breathing is complete.

Ask the MH to choose a classmate to turn the lights on.

Ask the MH to return to his or her seat.

1. **Introduce the lesson: Using deep belly breathing to help with anger.**

   Say: *Today we are going to be talking about breathing again. Paying attention to our breathing is a great way to practice mindfulness because our breath is always with us. We can't forget it, or leave it at home.*

   Today we are going to try doing something called deep belly breathing.

   Deep belly breathing is a great way to help you calm down when you are really mad, angry, sad or nervous.

   Raise your hand if you ever been really mad or angry. What does that feel like?

   Take a few answers.

   Ask: *What does your breath feel like when you are angry?*

   Take a few answers.

2. Demonstrate deep belly breathing. Use this script:

We have all felt angry before. Taking a few deep belly breaths can really help you feel like yourself again. And it's pretty easy once you get the hang of it! First watch me.

Place your hands on your belly and take a deep breath in through your nose and expand your belly as you breath in. Make it a little exaggerated so that they can see it. Exhale through your mouth and flatten your stomach. Do this is a few times.

Ask:

What did you notice about the way I was breathing? Did you see how my belly got bigger when I breathed in and flatter when I breathed out?

It's like I have a little balloon in my belly. When I breathe in I am filling the balloon full of air. When I breathe out I am emptying the balloon.

Let's get into our Mindful Bodies and try it together. Put your hands on your belly and take a deep breath in through your nose and try to imagine that you are filling the little balloon inside your belly with air.

Now breathe out slowly and gently through your mouth and imagine that you are emptying the balloon. Try that several times slowly and gently.

3. See your belly move

A great way to practice deep belly breathing is with a small object that can rest on a child's belly. You can use whatever you have around for this. One idea is small, flat river rocks about the size of silver dollars. You can use small stuffed animals if you have enough or bean bags. You want something heavy enough that the students are aware that there is something on their bellies but not so heavy that they have to work to lift it.

Say: *Now we are going to practice our deep belly breathing. The best and most fun way to practice this is while lying down.*

Ask for a volunteer to demonstrate. Have Susie lie down on her back in front of the class. Place the **small object** on her belly just above her belly button. Ask her to take a deep breath in through her nose and try to lift the object. Now ask her to take a nice slow deep breath out through her mouth and slowly lower the object. It might take her a while to get the hang of it. Ask the rest of the class to breathe along with her.

Next, you will be asking the class to lie on the floor. You might use these directions:

Now, are you ready to try it? Remember that this is a Mindfulness activity so we are going to be very quiet and calm while we are doing this. I am going to wait for everyone to find a place to lie down. Once I see that you are lying down with your body very still and your eyes closed, I am going to come around and put a small stone on your belly. Once you have the stone you can start practicing your deep belly breathing.

Go around and place the stones or other small objects on their bellies. This might take a while but it's a nice quiet moment, and the kids seem to enjoy lying down.

If this seems like it might make your children uncomfortable, you can have them keep their eyes open and focused on the ceiling.

Once everyone has their object you can ask them to breathe in unison.

Let's all take some deep belly breaths together. In and out, in and out, slowly and gently.

> *NOTE: When doing this exercise with something like river rocks, you may end by asking everyone to imagine what their rocks look like—color, shape, size. Then give them a chance to use their hands to feel the rock while keeping their eyes closed and to see what they can notice about the rock. They can rub it against their cheek and smell it too. Once they have spent some time mindfully touching the rock, they can sit up, open their eyes and look at their rocks. The kids really love this part.*

4. Encourage the children to practice their deep belly breathing when they go to bed at night with one of their own stuffed animals.

 Kindness Pals

Do the Kindness Pals activity as before. If you don't have time for the sharing, just assign the new Kindness Pals.

Closing: *Okay our time is up for today. Thank you for a great class, everyone. Let's have a nice quiet moment for the bell. If you want to, you can close your eyes, picture your new Kindness Pal, and imagine yourself doing something kind for them this week.*

Ring the bell.

Week 11
Brain Talk

OBJECTIVES:	Understand how two parts of our brain, the amygdala and the prefrontal cortex, operate in regulating our emotions and reactions to stimuli. Practice kindness.
PREPARE:	A bell or chime Arrange a way to show the video "Just Breathe" by Julia Bayer and Josh Saltzman to the whole class. Link: **https://www.YouTube.com/watch?v=RVA2N6tX2cg.** This lovely video shows children talking about how they feel when they get angry and how mindful breathing helps them to calm down. The video refers to two parts of the brain: the amygdala and the prefrontal cortex. Video of **Dr. Daniel Siegel's Hand Model** of the Brain. Watch this before class. This video is for the teacher, **not the students. http://www.drdansiegel.com/resources/everyday_mindsight_tools/** Diagram of the brain (found in Resource Section) Your Kindness Pals list and Talking Object

☺ Mindfulness Practice

Invite today's Mindfulness Helper (MH) to come to the front of the class to sit next to you on a chair.

Prompt the MH to choose another student to turn off the classroom lights.

Prompt the MH to say: "Let's get into our mindful bodies. Let's close our eyes. Let's take 3 deep breaths."

Say: *Let your breath settle back into its natural rhythm. You don't have to change it at all.*

While you are breathing, place your hand on your belly and feel the little move-ment that happens when your breath goes in and out.

Now move your hand to your chest and see what you feel there when your breath goes in and out. Try to notice where you felt your breath the most and keep your hand there, either on your belly or your chest.

Now we're going to count ten breaths. You can count them any way you want to. You can count one in-breath, or inhale, and one out-breath, or exhale, as one whole breath. Or you can count each inhale and exhale. It doesn't matter how you count them. Try to keep your mind focused on counting your breaths.

As soon as you notice that your mind has wandered away, try to bring it back to your counting starting again at one. Try not to count higher than ten. Once you get to ten, start over at one.

Okay, let's try it. Remember, this is just for fun. Don't worry if your mind wanders. Just try to bring it back when you notice it has wandered. Let's start now.

You can give them a minute or more to try this, whatever seems appropriate.

Okay, now you can stop focusing on your counting and let your mind be free to think or not think, whatever your mind wants to do.

Wait about 15 seconds.

Now let's take one more deep breath in and out. In a moment you will hear the sound of the bell and that will mean that it is time to open your eyes

Ask the MH to ring the bell.

Ask the MH to choose a classmate to turn the lights on.

Ask the MH to return to his or her seat.

1. **Show the class the video _Just Breathe_ (see link above).** 3 min 4 seconds.

2. **Discussion**

    *   Did you notice that one of the kids was talking about her brain?
    *   Did you notice she used some words you might not have heard before (amygdala and prefrontal cortex)?

3. **Use Dr. Daniel Siegel's hand model** of the brain to explain how the amygdala and the prefrontal cortex come into play when we are angry (see above).

    Say: _Today, we are going to be learning about out our brains. Did you know that your brain has many different parts? We are going to talk about two of them._

    Hold up your hand in the shape of the hand model.

    Can you do this with your hand? Tuck your thumb inside and then fold your fingers over your thumb. Now your hand looks a little bit like your brain.

    Hold your hand up next to your head.

    The first part is the Amygdala. The amygdala is the little part of your brain inside here.

    Lift your fingers to show the tucked-in thumb.

    The Amygdala

    The amygdala is the part of your brain that reacts to things. This is the part of the human brain that developed first. Even cave people had amygdalas. What kinds of things were the cave people worried about? Were they worried about being late for school or getting all of their homework done? (**They were worried about survival**.)

    Cave people were pretty much only worried about finding food and trying not to be somebody else's food. So their brains developed to help them with this.

    If cave man was walking through the forest and a saber-tooth tiger jumped out from behind a rock, what choices did he have? (**Run away or fight**.)

Those are the two things that amygdalas do best. The amygdala helps us decide in a flash whether to run away or try to kill the tiger. This is called the "fight or flight reflex."

When the Amygdala Overreacts

The fight or flight reflex was really helpful to early man and still helps to keep us safe. But sometimes it can overreact.

We can all think of times when our amygdala was in charge (when it would have been better if they weren't). If your Dad says you can't have ice cream after dinner, your amygdala says "No!! That's not fair! I WANT ICE CREAM!"

If you are playing basketball and somebody comes up and takes your ball, your amygdala says "Hey give it back!! It's mine!!" Your amygdala wants you to grab the ball back.

Ask: Can you think of a time when your amygdala told you to do or say something like that?

Your amygdala feels scared sometimes too. Your amygdala might tell you not to jump off the diving board or not to raise your hand in class to answer a hard question. Your amygdala might tell you not to try out for the travel soccer team or for a solo in a concert. But is not getting the solo in the concert the same thing as getting eaten by a saber tooth tiger? Nope. But your amygdala can't always tell the difference.

Ask: Can you think of a time when your amygdala was trying to protect you from something?

Your amygdala wants to take care of you, to protect you. But if we only listened to our amygdala, we wouldn't be very happy. We'd be in fights with people all of the time, and we wouldn't do anything that we are scared to do, even really fun things like learning how to ride a bike or learning how to dive.

The Prefrontal Cortex

Your amygdala wants to keep you safe. But humans have evolved to keep up with the changing world and our brains have evolved too.

We grew a new, very important part of our brains called the Prefrontal Cortex.

Fold your fingers back down.

This part (**pointing to your folded-over fingers**) *is called the Prefrontal Cortex. You can call it the PFC for short.*

Your Prefrontal Cortex is the part of your brain that helps you to make good decisions. It thinks things over and imagines what will happen.

Flipping Your Lid

Imagine that you are having a play date with a friend. You have a new Monopoly game and you can't wait to play. You've been looking forward to playing Monopoly all day. When your friend arrives she says that she has been cooped up inside all day and can't wait to go out to play soccer.

Ask the class:

- How do you feel? (Angry, upset, disappointed.)
- What does your amygdala tell you to do? (Cry, yell, tell her that if you can't play Monopoly, you'll hold your breath until you turn blue, …)
- How will things turn out if you only listen to your amygdala? (Your friend will be mad, might go home, won't want to play with you anymore…)

When we feel like that, it's as if we've flipped our lid.

Flip your fingers up exposing the amygdala.

It can feel like our amygdala is in charge, and we can't think very well because our Prefrontal Cortex or PFC is no longer working. You really need your Prefrontal Cortex (or PFC) to help you work this out. But how can you get it back in charge again?

When we take our deep breaths and take care of our anger, it helps to bring our Prefrontal Cortex back in charge.

Fold your fingers down slowly.

It can take a little while to work, but once we have our lids back on we can think about what we want to do. We have choices.

Putting the PFC Back In Charge

Once you have your lid back on and your PFC is in charge, you can think about how much you like your friend, and you start to think about your options.

Ask*: What are some other ways to solve this problem? (***Take turns playing soccer and Monopoly, let your guest decide what to play, and so on.***)*

Do you see how your PFC helps you see that you have choices and sometimes what your amygdala wants you to do isn't always the best idea?

Managing Our Anger

The next time you get angry, see if you can remember that this is your amygdala talking to you. See if you can use your breathing to help take care of your amygdala.

It's important to remember that your amygdala is trying to take care of you. If you feel angry or upset that is fine. All of your emotions are fine.

The problem with anger is that sometimes the way we express it can make things worse for us and for those around us.

Once you have calmed down, you can figure out the best way to express what is bothering you so that you can take care of it.

We are not trying to get rid of our anger or any of our emotions. We're just trying to make sure that our feelings aren't controlling us.

 ### Kindness Pals

Do the Kindness Pals activity as before. If you don't have time for the sharing just assign the new Kindness Pals.

Closing words: *Okay our time is up for today. Thank you for a great class, everyone. Let's have a nice quiet moment for the bell. If you want to, you can close your eyes, picture your new Kindness Pal, and imagine yourself doing something kind for them this week.*

Ring the bell.

Week 12
Brain Talk - Part 2

OBJECTIVES:	Understand how three parts of our brain, the amygdala, the hippocampus, and the prefrontal cortex, operate in regulating our emotions and reactions to stimuli.
	Practice kindness.
PREPARE:	A bell or chime
	Copies of *Rosie's Brain* Skit from the Resource Section
	Your Kindness Pals list and Talking Object

Mindfulness Practice

Invite today's Mindfulness Helper (MH) to come to the front of the class to sit next to you on a chair.

Prompt the MH to choose another student to turn off the classroom lights.

Prompt the MH to say: "Let's get into our mindful bodies. Let's close our eyes. Let's take five deep breaths."

Say: *Let's practice our Take Five breathing. Trace your hand while you breathe in and out five times.*

Say: *Now take a deep breath, and listen for the sound of the bell. When you hear that sound it will be time to open your eyes.*

Ask the MH to ring the bell.

Ask the MH to choose a classmate to turn the lights on.

Ask the MH to return to his or her seat.

1. **Introduce the Hippocampus**

   You might say:

   In this lesson we will be adding to our knowledge of the brain by learning about the Hippocampus. Do you remember last time when we learned about two parts of our brains?

   Can anybody remember what they were called or what they did?
   (**The amygdala and the prefrontal cortex.**)

   Review the jobs of the amygdala and the PFC.

   You might continue by saying:

   Well there are lots of other parts of your brain. Today we are going to learn about the Hippocampus. The hippocampus is like a big storage cabinet or a library inside of your brain. It is the part of the brain that stores all of your memories.

   Can anybody tell me you had for breakfast today? (**Let someone answer.**)

   Well that memory was stored in your hippocampus! Have you ever been to the beach? Eaten a pepper? Touched a snake? (**Let kids raise their hands if they have done any of those things.**)

   So when I asked those questions your brains went looking in the hippocampus for the answer. Some of us found it, but some of us we didn't because it was not there. Sometimes you forget something and that means that it was a little harder for your hippocampus to find it.

2. **Rosie's Brain Skit**

   Today we are going to act out a little skit that illustrates how these three parts of our brains work.

   Choose students to act out the Brain Skit found in Resource Section. You might act out the skit two or three times with different actors.

3. Discussion

You might ask:

- Why was Rosie's Amygdala angry?
- How did her Hippocampus help her?
- How did her PFC help her?
- Can you think of another solution to her problem?

 Kindness Pals

Do the Kindness Pals activity as before. If you don't have time for the sharing just assign the new Kindness Pals.

Closing words: *Okay our time is up for today. Thank you for a great class, everyone. Let's have a nice quiet moment for the bell. If you want to, you can close your eyes, picture your new Kindness Pal, and imagine yourself doing something kind for them this week.*

Ring the bell

Week 13
Noticing the Good Things

OBJECTIVES: To learn about our brain's tendency to focus on negative things more than positive.

Practice kindness.

PREPARE: A bell or chime

Your Kindness Pals list and Talking Object

Write this quote on the board: **"Every day may not be good but there is something good in every day."**
- Alice Morse Earle

 Mindfulness Practice

Invite today's Mindfulness Helper (MH) to come to the front of the class and sit next to you on a chair.

Prompt the MH to choose another student to turn off the classroom lights.

Prompt the MH to say: "Let's get into our mindful bodies. Let's close our eyes. Let's take 3 deep breaths."

Say: *Today I'd like you to try to remember a time when you were really happy. It could be something that just happened recently or something that you remember from a long time ago. Try to choose one time and when you're ready, try to travel back to that moment in your mind.*

Imagine that you are watching a movie of that happy moment and try to remember all of the details. Who were you with? Where were you? What happened? What made you so happy? What did it feel like to be happy? Where did you feel that happy feeling in your body?

Let's spend the next few moments (about 15 seconds) trying to stay in that happy moment. (Wait) Now let's travel back to this happy moment and listen for the sound of the bell.

Ask the MH to ring the bell.

Ask the MH to choose a classmate to turn the lights on.

Ask the MH to return to his or her seat.

Give students a chance to share some of their happy moments.

 1. Introduce the Negativity Bias

Say: *Do you remember what the role of the amygdala is? Let students answer.*

The role of the amygdala is to keep us safe. It is always looking out for threats to our safety. If we touch a cactus and get hurt, our brain will file that memory in order to prevent us from doing it again. That's helpful. Scientists call this the Negativity Bias.

This means that our brains tend to focus on and remember negative things more than positive things. Of course, we remember the big good things like our birthday, or a great trip, or a special event. But we often forget all about small good things.

For example, you might have invited five friends to your birthday party. At the last minute, one of your friends got sick and wasn't able to come. Instead of being happy that you have four friends to celebrate with, you might spend the whole day feeling sad that your one friend isn't there.

Have you ever been on vacation and after a day or two you start counting the days and start thinking, "Oh no, only four more days…." You might ruin your vacation because you are focused on the fact that it is going to end.

2. Overriding the Negativity Bias

Dr. Seuss said, "Don't cry because it's over. Smile because it happened."

This is a great way of thinking about how we can override our brain's Negativity Bias.

Scientists have found that a great way to balance out our brain's tendency to focus on negative things is to take a moment to soak in positive things. Taking time to notice and really focus on something good that happens allows our brains to send those memories to long-term storage. This is what we were doing during our mindfulness practice today.

Focusing on the positive doesn't mean that we are trying to avoid negative things. Not at all. Our brains will take care of that for us. By helping our brains recognize and soak in positive things we are helping our brains to see our lives more realistically. Maybe you slipped in mud during recess and your pants are all dirty. Sure, that's true and it's bad. But it's also true that your friends came running over and helped to clean you up and gave you a cookie after lunch to make you feel better. Your brain may only want to remember the mud, but by taking a mindful moment to remember and soak in the good feeling of having friends who care, you are helping to rewire your brain to recognize good things too. Let's give it a try.

3. Practice focusing on the positive

Let's close our eyes and take a deep breath. When you are ready I'd like you to try to make a list of good things that have happened in the past few days. These can be really small things like.... your Dad remembered not to put mayonnaise on your sandwich, your favorite pants were clean, you got picked to turn on the lights, your nose isn't stuffy.... just try to make a list.

Give them a minute or two to make a list.

Okay. Let's take one more deep breath in and out and open your eyes.

Give them a chance to share some of the good things on their list.

This is something that you can do every day. Maybe before you go to sleep every night you can make a list of the good things that happened that day. We can thank our amygdalas for watching out for us, but help our brains to see the good things that we might otherwise be missing.

 Kindness Pals

Do the Kindness Pal activity as before.

Closing words: Okay our time is up for today. Thank you for a great class, everyone.

Let's have a nice quiet moment for the bell. If you want to, you can close your eyes, picture your new Kindness Pal, and imagine yourself doing something kind for them this week.

Ring the bell.

Week 14
Gratitude Is Awesome

OBJECTIVES: Develop a sense of gratitude for the little things in life.

Become more mindful of the good that is always around us.

Practice kindness.

PREPARE: A bell or chime

The Book of Awesome by Neil Pasricha

The Book of Awesome is a really fun book, but *not everything in it is appropriate for kids*. Look through the book in advance and mark the pages that you can use in school. For example, "the smell of crayons", or "licking the batter off the beaters of a cake mixer," or "the sound of rain from inside a tent" or "the smell of freshly cut grass." Choose examples that your students will be able to relate to. Or create your own list and don't use the book.

Copies of the "Awesome Things" Worksheet for your class

Your Kindness Pals list and Talking Object

 Mindfulness Practice

Invite today's Mindfulness Helper (MH) to come to the front of the class to sit next to you on a chair.

Prompt the MH to choose another student to turn off the classroom lights.

Prompt the MH to say: "Let's get into our mindful bodies. Let's close our eyes. Let's take 3 deep breaths."

Say: *Today we are going to be thinking about gratitude or being thankful. I'd like you to think about that word "gratitude." I'd like you to ask yourself a question:* **"What or who am I grateful or thankful for right now?"**

Don't think about it too much but just notice what pops into your mind. Maybe you are grateful that it's almost time for recess, or that it isn't raining today, or that you have your favorite lunch waiting for you. Maybe you're thankful for having shoes that fit, socks that aren't itchy, or for having a friend to laugh with. Whatever it is that pops into your mind, just notice it.

Say: *Now take a deep breath, and listen for the sound of the bell. When you hear that sound it will be time to open your eyes.*

Ask the MH to ring the bell.

Ask the MH to choose a classmate to turn the lights on.

Ask the MH to return to his or her seat.

 1. Introduce the Gratitude Lesson

So last time we learned about our brain's Negativity Bias. We learned that because our amygdala is trying to keep us safe, it often focuses too much on negative things and tends to miss some of the little good things that are happening too.

We learned that one way to override your brain's Negativity Bias is to notice and focus on good things. Another word for this is Gratitude. When we are grateful for things, we notice them and feel thankful for them. Maybe you feel grateful because it's sunny out today. Maybe you are grateful that it is raining so that your garden will grow. Maybe you are grateful that your shoes are comfortable and not tight.

2. The Book of Awesome

Say: *There are also a million little things that we can be grateful for if we just stop to notice them. I'm going to share with you this cool book called* <u>The Book of Awesome</u> *that is filled with little awesome things.*

Read some examples aloud, or pass the book around and let the kids read the pages you've marked.

Ask the students to share their own "awesomes."

3. Worksheet and Sharing

Say: *Now I'm going to give you your new Kindness Pal and you two are going to work together to come up with a list of Ten Awesome Things. When everybody is done we'll share some of what is on our lists.*

Assign the new Pals.

Hand out the Ten Awesome Things worksheet. Give them about ten minutes to work on it and then time to share.

Kindness Pals

Since you have assigned the new pals already, you can skip this section, or just do the sharing.

Closing words: *Okay our time is up for today. Thank you for a great class, everyone.*

Let's have a nice quiet moment for the bell. If you want to, you can close your eyes, picture your new Kindness Pal, and imagine yourself doing something kind for them this week.

Ring the bell.

Peace of
Mind

Our List of Awesome Things

Names: _____

1. _____

2. _____

3. _____

4. _____

5. _____

6. _____

7. _____

8. _____

9. _____

10. _____

Week 15
Heartfulness

OBJECTIVES: **Use the practice of thinking kind thoughts to increase feelings of compassion and empathy for yourself and others.**

Practice kindness.

PREPARE: **A bell or chime**

Your Kindness Pals list and Talking Object

Heartfulness helps children strengthen their sense of compassion and empathy. It can also help them to let go of some angry feelings they have toward others.

 Mindfulness Practice

Invite today's Mindfulness Helper (MH) to come to the front of the class to sit next to you on a chair.

Prompt the MH to choose another student to turn off the classroom lights.

Prompt the MH to say: "Let's get into our mindful bodies. Let's close our eyes. Let's take 3 deep breaths."

Say: *Today we are going to do something called Heartfulness. This just means that we are going to be thinking about a person and sending them kind thoughts.*

But we aren't going to be making them a card or talking to them. We are going to be sending them kind thoughts in our minds.

I'd like you to think about someone who makes you happy. Someone you see every day, at home or at school, could be someone in your family, a friend, a teacher, even a pet. Just choose someone and try to picture them happy and smiling. Picture them doing something that makes them happy. … Try to notice how you feel when think about this person.

Now, if you'd like to, put your hand over your heart and repeat these words in your mind while you think about this person:

May you be happy. **Wait a moment.**

May you be healthy. **Wait a moment.**

May you be peaceful. **Wait a moment.**

Take a moment to notice how you feel. Any way that you feel is fine, even if you feel nothing. Just try to notice it.

This might feel a little strange, but this time we are going to send kind thoughts to ourselves. Imagine yourself happy and smiling, doing something that you like to do. Now repeat these words in your mind.

May I be happy. **Pause.**

May I be healthy. **Pause.**

May I be peaceful. **Pause**

Again, try to notice how you feel. Does it feel different to send kind thoughts to yourself? Any way that you feel is fine. Just try to notice it.

In a moment you will hear the sound of the bells and that will mean that it is time to open your eyes. So just get ready for that.

Ask the MH to ring the bell when the mindful breathing is complete.

Ask the MH to choose a classmate to turn the lights on.

Ask the MH to return to his or her seat.

Reflect and Discuss

Ask:

- What does it feel like to send kind thoughts to yourself?
- What does it feel like to send kind thoughts to others?

Say: *Sometimes practicing heartfulness can make us feel like being kinder to ourselves and to others.*

> *NOTE: Many children are uncomfortable sending kind thoughts to themselves thinking it makes them selfish.*
>
> *You can talk about the importance of treating ourselves with kindness and how we are often sending ourselves unkind thoughts throughout the day without even noticing it.*
>
> *You can remind the students that they can use heartfulness when they feel sad.*

Lesson Extension

You may invite the children to send heartfulness to sick or absent classmates.

 Kindness Pals

Do the Kindness Pals activity as before.

Closing: *Okay our time is up for today. Thank you for a great class, everyone. Let's have a nice quiet moment for the bell. If you want to, you can close your eyes, picture your new Kindness Pal, and imagine yourself doing something kind for them this week.*

Ring the bell

Week 16
Learn about Conflict with the Zax

OBJECTIVES: Learn what conflict means.

                Practice kindness.

PREPARE: A bell or chime

                "The Zax" by Dr. Seuss in <u>The Sneetches and
                Other Stories</u>

                Your Kindness Pals list and Talking Object

 Mindfulness Practice

Invite today's Mindfulness Helper (MH) to come to the front of the class to sit next to you on a chair.

Prompt the MH to choose another student to turn off the classroom lights.

Prompt the MH to say: "Let's get into our mindful bodies. Let's close our eyes. Let's take 3 deep breaths."

Say: *Let your breath settle back into its natural rhythm. You don't have to change it at all. Let's spend a few moments counting our breaths. Remember that if your mind wanders away from your breath, don't worry about it. Just gently bring your mind back to counting your breaths.*

Give them a minute or two to sit and quietly count. You can remind them once in a while to "notice where your mind is now."

Say: *Now let's take one more deep breath in and out. In a moment you will hear the sound of the bell and that will mean that it is time to open your eyes.*

Ask the MH to ring the bell when the mindful breathing is complete.

Ask the MH to choose a classmate to turn the lights on.

Ask the MH to return to his or her seat.

1. Introduce the lesson.

You might say:

Today we are going to learn a word that might be new to some of you.

Ask the class:

- Has anybody ever heard the word **Conflict** before?
- Does anybody have a guess about what it means?

Say:

In our Mindfulness lessons, we've been learning about what happens in our brains when we get angry. Well, sometimes when we are angry, it is because we have a conflict.

A conflict can be any kind of small problem. Maybe you are having a play date and you want to play outside but your friend wants to play inside. Maybe your little brother wants to play with you, but you want to read.

Conflicts can stay small or they can get bigger. Can anyone give an example of a conflict?

Today we are going to read a story that you have probably heard before. It is by the great Dr. Seuss.

You probably read his books when you were younger, but these books are not really books intended for little kids.

Dr. Seuss was a peacemaker and you have to be a little bit older to understand the real message in some of his stories. So try to hear this story as if you've never heard it before.

This story is called The Zax.

2. Read <u>The Zax</u>

After you read the story, **ask:**

- What is the conflict between the Zax?

- How you can you tell that they are getting angry? (Body language, yelling.)

- What part of the Zax's brains are controlling their actions? (Amygdala.)

- How is that choice working out for them?

3. Reflect

You might say and ask:

Luckily, we have more advanced brains than the Zax do.

What part of their brains would help them work this conflict out peacefully? (**The prefrontal cortex**.)

If they were using their PFCs, how could they solve this conflict?

4. Role Play

Introduce the Role Play. You might say:

Now we are going to act out the story of the Zax, but we are going to write new endings to the story.

I am going to ask two volunteers. One volunteer will pretend to be the North-Going Zax and the other will pretend to be the South-Going Zax.

The volunteers are going to act out a bit of the story, then they are going to come up with a better solution to the conflict.

Invite actors to act out the story, including their own solution.

The actors might suggest that one Zax leap frogs over the other so that no one has to go off of their chosen path. They might suggest that one goes through the other's legs.

If they don't suggest it, offer these ideas:

- They could take turns stepping out of the other's way each time they come around the world and meet in the same spot.

- One of them could just offer to step out of the way to let the other pass out of simple kindness.
- They could compromise so that they each agree to take one step to the side to let the other pass.

5. Discuss

Would things have turned out better for the Zax if they had tried any of our ideas?

 Kindness Pals

Do the Kindness Pals activity as before.

Closing: *Okay our time is up for today. Thank you for a great class, everyone. Let's have a nice quiet moment for the bell. If you want to, you can close your eyes, picture your new Kindness Pal, and imagine yourself doing something kind for them this week.*

Ring the bell

Week 17
The Conflict Escalator

OBJECTIVES: Use the concept of a **Conflict Escalator**, developed and named by William Kreidler, to help children understand how and why conflicts get worse. This is a key step in learning how to de-escalate conflicts and how to control behavior in conflict situations.

Practice kindness.

PREPARE: A bell or chime

Copies of the **Scrabble vs. Monopoly** Skits for all students (See Resource Section)

Your Kindness Pals list and Talking Object

☺ Mindfulness Practice

Invite today's Mindfulness Helper (MH) to come to the front of the class to sit next to you on a chair.

Prompt the MH to choose another student to turn off the classroom lights.

Prompt the MH to say: "Let's get into our mindful bodies. Let's close our eyes. Let's take 3 deep breaths."

Say: *Let your breath settle back into its natural rhythm. You don't have to change it at all. Let's spend a few moments counting our breaths. Remember that if your mind wanders away from your breath, don't worry about it. Just gently bring your mind back to counting your breaths.*

Give them a minute or two to sit and quietly count. You can remind them once in a while to "notice where your mind is now."

Say: *Now let's take one more deep breath in and out. In a moment you will hear the sound of the bell and that will mean that it is time to open your eyes.*

Ask the MH to ring the bell when the mindful breathing is complete.

Ask the MH to choose a classmate to turn the lights on.

Ask the MH to return to his or her seat.

 1. Introduce the Lesson

You might say:

Today we are going to continue talking about conflicts. Remember the story of the Zax? In that story the two creatures had a conflict—they each wanted to walk on the path and not have to step to one side.

Did their conflict stay small or did it get bigger?

What made their conflict get bigger? (The things that they said, the way that they said them, their stubbornness.)

One way to think about how conflicts get bigger is called the Conflict Escalator

2. Draw an escalator on the board. See the Resource Section for blank escalator that you may fill in. Refer to image at the end of this lesson for an example.

Ask the children to describe what an escalator does.

Explain that when a conflict gets worse, we say that the people involved are going up the Conflict Escalator.

Point out how the Zax went up the Conflict Escalator.

3. Scrabble vs. Monopoly 1

Hand out copies of the Skit. Say:

Today we are going to act out a skit about kids who are having a conflict. It's called: Scrabble v. Monopoly.

We will need six actors. They will be: Charlie, Henry, Julio, Lucy, Reign, and Alice.

The Scene is Charlie's house. The kids are having a play date.

Here is the *Scrabble vs. Monopoly 1* script you have handed out to the students:

Charlie: Hey guys, let's play Monopoly! I just got a new game, and I've been dying to play it.

Henry: That sounds great! I love Monopoly!

Julio: Yes! Monopoly is my favorite game!

Lucy: No way! Monopoly takes too long to play. Let's play Scrabble instead!

Reign: Yeah, Scrabble is awesome. I'm really good!

Alice: That's because you're a really good speller.

Reign: Thanks!

Charlie: What are you guys talking about? Monopoly is the coolest game. Scrabble is for geeks.

Lucy: Who are you calling a geek? You're a loser.

Henry: Yeah, Scrabble is boring. Only boring people like to play Scrabble.

Reign: If you guys are going to play Monopoly then Lucy and Alice and I are leaving!

Charlie: Fine with me! We don't like playing with dumb girls anyway!

Lucy, **Reign**, and **Alice** storm out.

4. **Discuss**

You might ask and explain like this:

Has this ever happened to you? You're having a good time and then suddenly everything gets out of control and goes totally wrong? This is called going up the Conflict Escalator.

Sometimes a conflict, problem, or argument can get worse and worse, and people start saying mean things, yelling, or even hitting each other. We call that going up the Conflict Escalator.

Questions for discussion:

- What was their conflict about?
- What was the first thing that made their conflict escalate or go up the Conflict Escalator?
- Then what happened? Let's map the conflict on the Conflict Escalator.
- What could these kids have done differently to avoid going up the Conflict Escalator?
- How could they work out this conflict?

Drawing on the lessons from Weeks 11 and 12, **ask**:

- What part of their brains are driving their reactions? (**Amygdala**.)
- Did the characters in the skit "flip their lids?" Give examples.

5. Scrabble vs. Monopoly 2

Invite new actors to assume the roles.

You might say: *Now let's act out another version of this skit and see what happens:*

Here are the lines for *Scrabble vs. Monopoly 2*.

Charlie: Hey guys, let's play Monopoly! I just got a new game and I've been dying to play it.

Henry: That sounds great! I love Monopoly!

Julio: Yes! Monopoly is my favorite game!

Lucy: No way! Monopoly takes too long to play. Let's play Scrabble instead!

Reign: Yeah, Scrabble is awesome. I'm really good!

Alice: That's because you're a really good speller.

Reign: Thanks!

Charlie: What are you talking about? Monopoly is the coolest game. Scrabble is for geeks!

Lucy: Who are you calling a geek? You're a loser.

Henry: Hey you guys, we're going up the Conflict Escalator.

Reign: Oh, you're right. There's nothing but trouble at the top of the Conflict Escalator!

Julio: Why don't we calm down a bit? Let's do our Take Five breathing.

Everybody stops and traces their hands while slowly breathing in and out.

Lucy: Hey, Charlie, I'm sorry I called you a loser. I didn't mean it.

Charlie: No, I'm sorry. I shouldn't have said Scrabble is for geeks. I like Scrabble. I was just really excited to play Monopoly and I got carried away.

Alice: I have an idea! Why don't we take turns. We can play Monopoly today and then tomorrow we can go over to my house and play Scrabble.

All: That's a great idea!

The End

6. **Discuss**

You might ask:

- Do you think that was a good way to work out their conflict?
- Was it better than going up the Conflict Escalator?

When people go up the Conflict Escalator someone always gets hurt. Either their feelings get hurt or they get hurt physically.

Ask:

- How did the kids calm down? (**Breathing.**)
- Did taking those deep breaths help them to quiet their amygdalae?
- What part of their brains was in charge when they worked out the conflict peacefully? (**Prefrontal cortex.**)
- What else did they do to bring their conflict down the Escalator? (**Apologize.**)

Okay, next time we are going to act out another skit about the Conflict Escalator.

 Kindness Pals

Do the Kindness Pals activity as before. If you don't have time for sharing, just assign the new Kindness Pals.

Closing: *Okay our time is up for today. Thank you for a great class, everyone. Let's have a nice quiet moment for the bell. If you want to, you can close your eyes, picture your new Kindness Pal, and imagine yourself doing something kind for them this week.*

Ring the bell.

Week 18
Conflict Escalator Practice: The Class Party

OBJECTIVES: Reinforce the concept of the Conflict Escalator and
                   lay the foundation for the Conflict CAT.

                   Practice kindness.

PREPARE: A bell or chime

                   Copies of the skits *The Class Party 1* and *The Class
                   Party 2* found in Resource Section

                   Your Kindness Pals list and Talking Object

 Mindfulness Practice

Say: *Today we are going to start out by practicing Heartfulness. This just
means that we are going to be thinking about a person and sending them kind
thoughts. We did this a while back so you might remember it.*

Invite the day's Mindfulness Helper (MH) to come to the front of the class to
sit next to you on a chair.

Prompt the MH to choose another student to turn off the classroom lights.

Prompt the MH to say: "Let's get into our mindful bodies. Let's close our
eyes. Let's take 3 deep breaths."

Say: *I'd like you to think about someone who makes you happy. Choose
someone you see every day, at home or at school. It could be someone in your
family, a friend, a teacher, even a pet. Just choose someone and try to picture
this person happy and smiling. Picture them doing something that makes them
happy. Try to notice how you feel when you think about this person.*

*Now, if you'd like to, fill your heart up with kindness and repeat these words in
your mind while you think about this person:*

May you be happy. **Wait a moment.**

May you be healthy. **Wait a moment.**

May you be peaceful. **Wait a moment.**

|

Take a moment to notice how you feel. Any way that you feel is fine, even if you feel nothing. Just try to notice it.

Introduce a new focus: *Now we are going to try this again but this time we are going to send kind thoughts to someone that we are angry with or in a conflict with. This might be harder but just try it and see what happens.*

Now, if you'd like to, fill your heart up with kindness and repeat these words in your mind while you think about this person:

May you be happy. **Wait a moment.**

May you be healthy. **Wait a moment.**

May you be peaceful. **Wait a moment.**

Take a moment to notice how you feel. Any way that you feel is fine, even if you feel nothing. Just try to notice it.

Say: *Now let's take one more deep breath in and out. In a moment you will hear the sound of the bell and that will mean that it is time to open your eyes.*

Ask the MH to ring the bell when the mindful breathing is complete.

Ask the MH to choose a classmate to turn the lights on.

Ask the MH to return to his or her seat.

Invite the students to share what it was like to send kind thoughts in your mind to someone you are angry with or in a conflict with. **Ask them not to share the names of the person they were thinking about if it is someone at school.**

 1. Introduce the Lesson

You might say:

In our last class we learned about the Conflict Escalator. Does anybody remember what that is?

We acted out a skit about kids having a conflict about what game to play.

Today we are going to act out another skit about a conflict. It's called The Class Party. I will be choosing some people to play the parts in the skit.

I want the rest of you to pay close attention and every time you notice some-body doing or saying something that causes the conflict to escalate or go up the Conflict Escalator I want you to point up. When you notice somebody doing something that causes the conflict to go down the Conflict Escalator, point down.

2. The Class Party Skit: Version One

We will need five actors. They will be: Richard, Leslie, Carlos, Diana and Oscar.

Choose Actors.

The Scene is a school classroom during indoor recess.

Hand out copies of the *Class Party 1* Skit.

The Class Party 1

Richard: I'm so excited about this party!

Oscar: Yeah, me too. I can't believe the teacher is letting us come up with the theme.

Carlos: I know, it's going to be awesome! I think we should have a choco-late theme. We could fill the entire classroom with chocolate and just swim around in it for the whole day!

All: Carlos!

Diana: Carlos, that is a ridiculous idea. Although it does sound like fun. We have to come up with something the teacher will actually let us do.

Leslie: How about a craft party? We could set up lots of stations and make a bunch of different crafts.

Richard: Nah, that sounds boring. All you ever want to do is make little crafty things. I think we should have a Star Wars theme.

Oscar: Yeah, we could have huge light saber fights!

Carlos: Cool! And the light sabers could be made of chocolate.

All: Carlos!

Diana: Not everybody likes Star Wars and the fighting sounds too violent. How about a Harry Potter party?

Leslie: I love Harry Potter!

Oscar: Harry Potter is stupid—I hate all that magic stuff.

Diana: Harry Potter isn't stupid. You're stupid!

Richard: We're never going to agree on a party theme. You girls have such dumb girlie ideas. I wouldn't come to any party that you planned.

Oscar: Me neither.

Diana: Well, fine. I wouldn't come to your stinky party either. Maybe the teacher will let us have separate parties.

Leslie: That would be great—that way we don't have to talk to you anymore.

Richard and Oscar and Carlos: Fine with us!

Everyone storms out.

3. **Discuss**

You might say:

Does this sound familiar? You're just talking and then everything gets out of control. Sometimes you're not even sure what happened. All you know is that you're mad.

Ask:

- What was their conflict about? What happened that caused their conflict to escalate, get worse, or go up the Conflict Escalator?
- What part of the brain is responsible for making us go up the Conflict Escalator?

- Are these kids being mindful of what they are saying? What did you think they should do to try to bring their conflict down the Conflict Escalator?

Now we're going to act out another version of this skit. Let's see what happens when they try things a different way:

4. **The Class Party Skit: Version 2**

Hand out Copies of *Class Party 2* Skit.

Invite new actors to assume the roles.

You might say: *Now let's act out another version of this skit and see what happens:*

The Class Party 2

Richard: I'm so excited about this party!

Oscar: Yeah, me too. I can't believe the teacher is letting us come up with the theme.

Carlos: I know! It's going to be awesome! I think we should have a chocolate theme. We could fill the entire classroom with chocolate and just swim around in it for the whole day!

All: Carlos!

Diana: Carlos, that is a ridiculous idea. Although it does sound like fun. We have to come up with something the teacher will actually let us do.

Leslie: How about a craft party? We could set up lots of stations and make a bunch of different crafts.

Richard: Nah, that sounds boring. All you ever want to do is make little crafty things. I think we should have a Star Wars theme.

Oscar: Yeah, we could have huge light saber fights!

Carlos: Cool! And the light sabers could be made of chocolate.

All: Carlos!

Diana: Not everybody likes Star Wars and the fighting sounds too violent. How about a Harry Potter party?

Leslie: I love Harry Potter!

Oscar: Harry Potter is stupid—I hate all that magic stuff.

Diana: Harry Potter isn't stupid. You're stupid!

Leslie: Hang on, we're going up the Conflict Escalator! If we keep fighting, we're never going to come up with an idea, and we might not get to have the party;

Richard: She's right. We need to calm down. Let's take some deep breaths.

Everybody takes three slow deep breaths.

Diana: I'm sorry I said you are stupid, Oscar. I really didn't mean it. I was just flipping my lid.

Oscar: I'm sorry too. Harry Potter isn't stupid.

Richard: And I'm sorry I said that a craft party would be boring. That was mean. I actually like making stuff, I just didn't want the whole party to be crafts.

Leslie: That's okay.

Carlos: How about having a "Go Green" party? We all care about the environment. We could make posters to put up around the school reminding people to recycle and stuff.

Diana: And we could make birdfeeders out of pine cones and peanut butter and birdseed.

Richard: Cool! And we could even make light sabers out of recycled paper towel rolls.

Carlos: And we could have a dunk tank filled with chocolate!

All: Carlos!!!

Everybody high fives each other.

5. Discuss

Do you think that was a good way to work out their conflict? What is another idea? What else did you notice that they did to bring their conflict down?

Next time we are going to be talking about apologizing.

 Kindness Pals

Do the Kindness Pals activity as before. If you don't have time for sharing, just assign the new Kindness Pals.

Closing: *Okay our time is up for today. Thank you for a great class, everyone. Let's have a nice quiet moment for the bell. If you want to, you can close your eyes, picture your new Kindness Pal, and imagine yourself doing something kind for them this week.*

Ring the bell.

Week 19
Apologizing

OBJECTIVES: Discuss how a proper apology can help to defuse a conflict.

Practice kindness.

PREPARE: A bell or chime

<u>Sorry</u> by Trudy Ludwig

Your Kindness Pals list and Talking Object

 Mindfulness Practice

Invite today's Mindfulness Helper (MH) to come to the front of the class to sit next to you on a chair.

Prompt the MH to choose another student to turn off the classroom lights.

Prompt the MH to say: "Let's get into our mindful bodies. Let's close our eyes. Let's take 3 deep breaths."

Say: *Let's keep our eyes closed. I'd like you to try to remember a time when you did something that hurt somebody else's feelings. It happens to all of us. Try to remember a time.* **Pause**

How did you feel? What did you do about it? Did you say you were sorry? Was that hard? **Pause**

If you didn't say you were sorry try saying it now. You can whisper it or say it inside your mind. **Pause**

Say: *Now let's take one more deep breath in and out. In a moment you will hear the sound of the bell and that will mean that it is time to open your eyes.*

Ask the MH to ring the bell.

Ask the MH to choose a classmate to turn the lights back on.

Ask the MH to return to his or her seat.

Ask: *Does anybody want to share what you were thinking about?*

Say: *Is it hard to say you're sorry?*

Today we are going to read a story about saying "I'm Sorry" or apologizing.

1. Introduce the Lesson

You might say:

When two or more people go up the conflict escalator, everyone involved has done something to escalate the conflict. You can't go up the conflict escalator alone.

In order to come to a fair and long-lasting solution it is important that everyone takes responsibility for their actions and their part in making the conflict escalate.

The act of apologizing for whatever you did, like "I'm sorry I called you a jerk" or "I'm sorry I said your idea was boring," can clear the air and make it much easier for you to see the other person's point of view and find a fair solution.

2. Read the book <u>Sorry!</u>

3. Discuss

Discuss what makes a good apology.

The formula included in this book—Regret, Remedy, Responsibility—can be too difficult for children to understand.

You may use this simpler version instead: **Mean it, Own it, Fix it.**

 Kindness Pals

Do the Kindness Pals activity as before. If you don't have time for sharing, just assign the new Kindness Pals.

Closing words: *Okay, our time is up for today. Thank you for a great class, everyone. Let's have a nice quiet moment for the bell. If you want to, you can close your eyes, picture your new Kindness Pal, and imagine yourself doing something kind for them this week.*

Ring the bell.

Week 20
Introduce the Conflict CAT

OBJECTIVES: Introduce a new Conflict Resolution method.
Practice kindness.

PREPARE: A bell or chime
Copy of the Conflict CAT for the classroom
Your Kindness Pals list and Talking Object

 Mindfulness Practice

Invite today's Mindfulness Helper (MH) to come to the front of the class to sit next to you on a chair.

Prompt the MH to choose another student to turn off the classroom lights.

Prompt the MH to say "Let's get into our mindful bodies. Let's close our eyes. Let's take 3 deep breaths."

Say: *Let your breath settle back into its natural rhythm. You don't have to change it at all. Let's spend a few moments counting our breaths.*

Remember that if your mind wanders away from your breath, don't worry about it. Just gently bring your mind back to counting your breaths.

Give them a minute or two to sit and quietly count. You can remind them once in a while to "notice where your mind is now."

Now let's take one more deep breath in and out. In a moment you will hear the sound of the bell and that will mean that it is time to open your eyes.

Ask the MH to ring the bell.

Ask the MH to choose a classmate to turn the lights on.

Ask the MH to return to his or her seat.

1. Introduce the Lesson

Review what you have already done. You might say:

So far we have learned about what conflict is and how it escalates or goes up the Conflict Escalator. We've also learned about good ways to apologize. And in our mindfulness lessons, we've learned many ways to help us to calm down when we are angry.

We've learned about what happens in our brains when we get angry, how we flip our lids and we let our amygdala take over.

This is really powerful information that most people, including most grown-ups, don't have. With these tools we can make our own lives easier and make the world a more peaceful place.

Introduce the Conflict CAT

Today we are going to put all of these pieces together in a fun way that is easy to remember. I'd like to introduce you to the **Conflict CAT** *The Conflict CAT stands for the three most important things to do to work out a conflict:*

> **C**alm down
> **A**pologize
> **T**oolbox

We've already learned about the first two parts. Today we are going to start to learn about what is in the Conflict Toolbox.

Introduce the Toolbox: Taking Turns, Sharing and Being Kind

Remember the skit we saw about the kids who were fighting over whether to play Monopoly or Scrabble?

Does anybody remember how they worked out their conflict? (They calmed down, they apologized, and then they decided to take turns.)

Taking turns *is one of the tools in the Conflict Toolbox. Taking turns is a great tool to use and it works for a lot of conflicts. Let's say you need to use the classroom computer for a project, but someone is already using it to play a game. Would taking turns be a tool that would work to solve that conflict?*

90 | | http://www.teachpeaceofmind.com

What if you were planning to play basketball with your friends at recess, but when you get out to the playground some other kids are already there playing? Would taking turns work in that situation?

What it if you and your brother really wanted to eat a cupcake, but there was only one cupcake left? Would taking turns work in that situation? First you eat the cupcake and then your brother eats it? Maybe not.

*What would be a good tool to use in that situation? Yes, you could **share** it. Or you could just let your brother eat the cupcake. That's a tool we call "**being kind.**" So one tool doesn't work in every situation, but that's okay because there are a lot more!*

2. Using the Toolbox

Ask the class to apply these tools to different situations you suggest.

You might say:

*Today we are going to focus on three tools: **taking turns, sharing**, and **being kind**. I'm going to describe a conflict, and I want you to tell me which tool would work the best and why.*

Suggest these situations and ask which tools the class would use.

- You and your friend both want to go first in a game.
- You and a classmate both want to sit in the class rocking chair.
- You want to draw but somebody is already using all of the markers.
- You and a friend can't agree on a movie to watch.
- You and your sister are doing homework and you both need to use the family computer.

3. Looking ahead

Next time we are going to learn more tools and practice using them. Explain to the class that you are going to be learning a three-step process to work out conflicts.

Kindness Pals

Do the Kindness Pals activity as before. If you don't have time for sharing, just assign the new Kindness Pals.

Closing words: *Okay, our time is up for today. Thank you for a great class, everyone. Let's have a nice quiet moment for the bell. If you want to, you can close your eyes, picture your new Kindness Pal, and imagine yourself doing something kind for them this week.*

Ring the bell.

More about the Conflict Toolbox

OBJECTIVES:	Introduce more tools to help work out conflicts.
	Practice kindness.
PREPARE:	A bell or chime
	Copies of the *Monopoly vs. Scrabble 1* Skit from Resource Section
	Your Kindness Pals list and Talking Object

 Mindfulness Practice

Invite today's Mindfulness Helper (MH) to come to the front of the class to sit next to you on a chair.

Prompt the MH to choose another student to turn off the classroom lights.

Prompt the MH to say: "Let's get into our mindful bodies. Let's close our eyes. Let's take 3 deep breaths."

Say: *Let your breath settle back into its natural rhythm. You don't have to change it at all. Let's spend a few moments counting our breaths. Remember that if your mind wanders away from your breath, don't worry about it. Just gently bring your mind back to counting your breaths.*

Give them a minute or two to sit and quietly count. You can remind them once in a while to "notice where your mind is now."

Say: *Now let's take one more deep breath in and out. In a moment you will hear the sound of the bell and that will mean that it is time to open your eyes.*

Ask the MH to ring the bell.

Ask the MH to choose a classmate to turn the lights on.

Ask the MH to return to his or her seat.

1. Introduce the Lesson

Review the Conflict CAT and introduce the remaining 5 tools.

You might say:

Today we are going to learn about more of the tools in the Conflict CAT

Remember that the Conflict CAT stands for the three most important things to do to work out a conflict: Calm down, Apologize, Toolbox.

*Last time we learned about three tools: **Share**, **Take Turns**, and **Be Kind**.*

There are eight tools in the Conflict Toolbox. There are so many other ways to work out conflicts, but these are eight that come in pretty handy. They are:

1. **Share**
2. **Take Turns**
3. **Be Kind**
4. **Leave it to Chance**

5. **Compromise**
6. **Pause the Conflict**
7. **Skip the Conflict**
8. **Get Help**

2. Review each Tool

Share these descriptions of each tool with the class.

Leave it to Chance

Leave it to chance might sound strange, but it's the one you've probably used the most. Leaving it to chance can mean flipping a coin, playing rock, paper, scissors, or something else like that.

Leaving it to chance can be a great tool to use, but there are some drawbacks.

What often happens when we flip a coin to work out a conflict? That's right, the person who loses the coin toss might say "Let's do best two out of three, or three out of five…"

I suggest that when you use this tool, you check in with everyone first and make sure that everyone is okay with losing.

If you are having a conflict over something that is really important to you or over something that you have to do, this might not be the best tool to use. If you are having a conflict over who gets to use your family computer and you both have homework to do on the computer, is flipping a coin going to work? No, because then one of you won't get to do your homework. So we need more tools…

Compromise

Another important tool is <u>Compromise</u>. A compromise means that nobody in the conflict gets exactly what he or she wants, but both people agree on a solution in which they both get something good.

Let's say that you and your brother both want that last cookie in the cookie jar. A compromise would be that neither one of you eats the cookie, but that you eat some ice cream instead. As long as you both like ice cream, then that's a good compromise.

Pausing the Conflict

<u>Pausing the Conflict</u> means that you realize that you are going up the Conflict Escalator but that it is going to take you a bit longer to calm down enough to work out the conflict. Maybe you need to go to your room for a little while to do your mindful breathing. Maybe you need to go for a walk and count your steps and take care of your anger. Once you've calmed down, you can come back together and try to work things out.

Skip the Conflict

Sometimes a conflict just isn't worth going up the Conflict Escalator for. There is nothing but TROUBLE at the top of the Conflict Escalator. Once you have taken some deep breaths and calmed down a bit, you might realize that you are having a conflict about something silly. So you decide to <u>Skip the Conflict</u>.

This is a good tool to use also when you realize that you are doing your best to calm down and use the Conflict CAT, but you notice that the other person is still really angry and wanting to go up the Conflict Escalator. That would be a good time to walk away and <u>Skip the Conflict</u>.

Get Help

Sometimes when you are trying to work out a conflict you might need to <u>Get Help</u>. That means that you might ask a grown-up or a friend to help you work things out. Sometimes it's hard to see the solution when you are in the middle of something. If you are trying to be calm and work things out but the other person has flipped their lid, that would be a good time to <u>Get Help</u> too.

3. **Putting Tools to Work: Monopoly Skit**

You might say:

Do you remember the two skits that we acted out about conflicts? There was one about a group of kids arguing about playing Monopoly or Scrabble. There was one about a group of kids trying to come up with a theme for their class party.

*Looking at the list of tools in the Conflict Toolbox, which tool did the kids use in the Monopoly skit? (**Take turns.**) That's right, they decided to take turns and play Monopoly today and Scrabble tomorrow.*

*What tool did the kids use in the class party skit? (**Compromise.**) Since they all had different ideas for what the party should be, they came up with a compromise. They thought of something that they all cared about—the environment—and planned a party about that.*

What other tools would have worked in these conflicts? Let's act out the Monopoly skit again, but this time we are going to stop before they are done and see what other tool could work. We're going to read through the skit but then at the end I'm going to ask you to improvise or make up what the kids would say. Let's try it:

Hand out copies of the *Scrabble vs. Monopoly* Skit.

Choose 6 volunteers to play the roles of Charlie, Henry, Julio, Lucy, Reign and Alice.

Charlie: Hey guys, let's play Monopoly! I just got a new game and I've been dying to play it.

Henry: That sounds great! I love Monopoly!

Julio: Yes! Monopoly is my favorite game!

Lucy: No way! Monopoly takes too long to play. Let's play Scrabble instead!

Reign: Yeah, Scrabble is awesome. I'm really good!

Alice: That's because you're a really good speller.

Reign: Thanks!

Charlie: What are you talking about? Monopoly is the coolest game. Scrabble is for geeks!

Lucy: Who are you calling a geek? You're a loser.

Henry: Hey you guys, we're going up the Conflict Escalator.

Reign: Oh, you're right. There's nothing but trouble at the top of the Conflict Escalator!

Julio: Why don't we calm down a bit? Let's do our Take Five breathing.

Everybody stops and traces their hands and takes five deep breaths.

Lucy: Hey, Charlie, I'm sorry I called you a loser. I didn't mean it.

Charlie: No, I'm sorry. I shouldn't have said Scrabble is for geeks. I like Scrabble. I was just really excited to play Monopoly and I got carried away.

Alice: I have an idea! ***STOP HERE***

3. Discuss and Repeat

What tool in the toolbox would work to solve this conflict?

Take some ideas and then choose one to have the kids act out.

Talk about how it worked.

Repeat a few times to try out different tools.

Kindness Pals

Do the Kindness Pals activity as before. If you don't have time for sharing, just assign the new Kindness Pals.

Closing words: *Okay, our time is up for today. Thank you for a great class, everyone. Let's have a nice quiet moment for the bell. If you want to, you can close your eyes, picture your new Kindness Pal, and imagine yourself doing something kind for them this week.*

Ring the bell.

Week 22
Conflict CAT Role Play 1

OBJECTIVES: Practice the Conflict Resolution skills taught in previous lessons.

                                  Practice kindness.

PREPARE: A bell or chime

                                    Copy "Conflict CAT Role Play Scenarios" (at end of lesson) and cut into strips. Alternatively, you may write your own conflicts on slips of paper or index cards.

                                    Have a poster of the Conflict Escalator, the Conflict CAT, and the Toolbox up where the kids can see them. See Resource Section

                                    Your Kindness Pals list and talking object

 Mindfulness Practice

Invite today's Mindfulness Helper (MH) to come to the front of the class to sit next to you on a chair.

Prompt the MH to choose another student to turn off the classroom lights.

Prompt the MH to say: "Let's get into our mindful bodies. Let's close our eyes. Let's take 3 deep breaths."

Say: *Today we are going to take a little trip around our bodies with our minds.*

I want you to start by thinking about the top of your head. Imagine that you can touch the top of your head, not with your hand, but with your mind. It's like you're touching the top of your head from the inside. Can you feel anything when you focus your mind on the top of your head? **Pause**.

Now let's travel down into our faces. Try to feel your forehead—does it feel tight and scrunched? What does it feel like if you try to make it feel more relaxed and smooth? Notice your mouth—is it hanging loose and down? Notice what it feels like if you smile a little bit. **Pause.** *Try to notice your ears—can you feel* *your ears with your mind? Let's travel down to your neck and shoulders. Notice if your shoulders are tight and high. What does it feel like if you soften and lower your shoulders a bit?* **Pause.**

Let the attention travel down your right arm all the way down to your fingers. Do you remember how your hands felt after you clapped them together? Does your hand feel different now? What do you notice? Let your attention travel down your other arm to your other hand. What do you notice there? Now let your mind travel down your back. Is your back nice and straight or are you hunched over? Notice what it feels like to have a nice, straight back.

Notice the weight of your body on the chair or on the rug or cushion. Let your mind travel down your legs. Do your legs feel the same or different from each other? Try to pay attention to each one of your toes. Give them a little wiggle. Now bring your attention back up to the top of your head and try to sweep down through your whole body. Which foot is warmer?

Now listen for the sound of the bell. When you hear that sound it will be time to open your eyes.

Signal the MH to ring the bell.

Ask the MH to choose a classmate to turn the lights on.

Ask the MH to return to his or her seat.

1. Review Conflict Escalator, what makes a good apology, and the Conflict Resolution Toolbox.

So we've learned a lot about working out conflicts so far. We've learned about how to use our breathing to help us to Calm Down. We've learned about how to apologize well. We've learned eight tools to use to work out conflicts. So let's see if we can put it all together.

2. Introduce the Lesson

You might say:

Today I'm going to ask you to work with your Kindness Pal (**or assign a partner**).

I am going to give each of you a conflict to work out in a role play. You'll have a few minutes to work out how you are going to do it and to think about which tool you are going to use. Make sure that your role play shows all the parts of the Conflict CAT

*You can show us how you go up the Conflict Escalator a little bit (**this is fun**), but then we want to see how you come down.*

One of you has to say "Uh oh, we're going up the Conflict Escalator." You have to show that you are taking some deep breaths. At least one of you has to apologize.

Then you need to show us that you are using one of the tools in the Toolbox.

The rules are: no bad language and no touching each other. Agreed?

When time is up, I'll choose some pairs to come up and show us what you've done.

3. **Role Plays**

When everyone is paired up, pass out the conflicts and ring a bell. Ring it again when time is up. Be flexible with the time.

> *NOTE: The real learning is coming from this part of the process so don't rush it.*

After you ring the bell, ask some kids to come up and show the class what they've come up with.

Make sure that they have covered all of the Conflict CAT steps.

Conflicts on slips (see following page):

- Two kids are arguing about what to name the class guinea pig.
- Two kids are arguing over who gets to walk the new puppy first.
- Two kids can't agree on what kind of restaurant to go to with their family.
- Two kids argue over whether to play football or go on the monkey bars during recess.
- Two kids argue over what kind of pet to get.
- Two kids argue about whether pie or cake is better.
- Two kids argue over whose turn it is to sit on the class bean bag chair.
- Two kids argue about who gets to use the family computer.
- Two kids argue about what to watch on TV.
- Two kids argue over who gets to check out a new library book.
- Two kids argue over what is the best ice cream flavor.
- Two kids argue over whether biking is better than swimming.

 Kindness Pals

Do the Kindness Pals activity as before. If you don't have time for sharing, just assign the new Kindness Pals.

Closing words: *Okay, our time is up for today. Thank you for a great class, everyone. Let's have a nice quiet moment for the bell. If you want to, you can close your eyes, picture your new Kindness Pal, and imagine yourself doing something kind for them this week.*

Ring the bell.

Conflict CAT Role Play Scenarios

Copy and cut apart to hand to your students.

✂---

Two kids are arguing about what to name the class guinea pig.

Two kids can't agree on what kind of restaurant to go to with their family.

Two kids argue over whether to play football or go on the monkey bars during recess.

Two kids argue over what kind of pet to get.

Two kids argue about whether pie or cake is better.

Two kids argue over whose turn it is to sit on the class bean bag chair.

Two kids argue about who gets to use the family computer.

Two kids argue about what to watch on TV.

Two kids argue over who gets to check out a new library book.

Two kids argue over what is the best ice cream flavor.

Two kids argue over whether biking is better than swimming.

Week 23
Conflict CAT Role Play 2  ≫REPEAT ME≫

OBJECTIVES: To reinforce the Conflict CAT through role playing.

Practice kindness.

PREPARE: A bell or chime

Display posters of the Conflict Escalator, the Conflict CAT, and the Toolbox where kids can see them (see Resource Section)

Your Kindness Pals list and Talking Object

 Mindfulness Practice

Invite today's Mindfulness Helper (MH) to come to the front of the class to sit next to you on a chair.

Prompt the MH to choose another student to turn off the classroom lights.

Prompt the MH to say: "Let's get into our mindful bodies. Let's close our eyes. Let's take 3 deep breaths."

Say: *Let your breath settle back into its natural rhythm. You don't have to change it at all. Let's spend a few moments counting our breaths. Remember that if your mind wanders away from your breath, don't worry about it. Just gently bring your mind back to counting your breaths.*

Give them a minute or two *to sit and quietly count. You can remind them once in a while to "notice where your mind is now."*

Say: *Now let's take one more deep breath in and out. In a moment you will hear the sound of the bell and that will mean that it is time to open your eyes.*

Ask the MH to ring the bell.

1. Introduce the Lesson

In this lesson, students will create their own conflict and conflict resolution. Their process should reflect all of the parts of the Conflict CAT and the Conflict Escalator.

This type of practice is essential if the students are to develop the ability to use these tools in real situations.

You might say:

Today we are going to be role-playing again. But this time you are going to create your own conflict. Just like last time, your skit needs to show all the parts of the Conflict CAT You can show us how you go up the Conflict Escalator a little bit (this is fun), but then we want to see how you come down.

One of you has to say: "Uh oh, we're going up the Conflict Escalator."

You have to show that you are taking some deep breaths.

At least one of you has to apologize.

Then you need to show us that you are using one of the tools in the Toolbox.

Make sure that your conflict is realistic and appropriate.

The rules are no bad language and no touching each other. Okay?

When time is up I'll choose some pairs to come up and show us what you've done.

2. Role Plays

Walk around and check in with each pair. Key points to emphasize:

- Make sure that they are role-playing something appropriate and realistic.
- Ask them what tool they are planning to use.
- Encourage them not to spend much time going up the Conflict Escalator but rather to focus on coming down.

Kindness Pals

Do the Kindness Pals activity as before. If you don't have time for sharing, just assign the new Kindness Pals.

Closing words: *Okay, our time is up for today. Thank you for a great class, everyone. Let's have a nice quiet moment for the bell. If you want to, you can close your eyes, picture your new Kindness Pal, and imagine yourself doing something kind for them this week.*

Ring the bell.

Week 24
Peaceful Place >>REPEAT ME>>

OBJECTIVES: Learn the skill of visualization to calm down and focus.

Practice kindness.

PREPARE: A bell or chime

Your Kindness Pals list and Talking Object

> NOTE: *Visualization is a fun way to practice mindfulness that the children really enjoy. Focusing your mind on a peaceful place can help you to calm down, to focus your mind, to think about your senses, and to really settle yourself into the moment, even if it is in your imagination.*
>
> *Please consider the composition of your class when you offer examples of Peaceful Places a student might call to mind. It could be a real place, an imaginary place, a vacation memory, or a local park.*

 1. Choose a Mindfulness Helper

Consult your alphabetical roll list, and choose the next student to be the Mindfulness Helper for the day.

Invite today's Mindfulness Helper (MH) to come to the front of the class to sit next to you on a chair.

Prompt the MH to choose another student to turn off the classroom lights.

Prompt the MH to say: "Let's get into our mindful bodies. Let's close our eyes. Let's take 3 deep breaths."

2. **Guide the children through a visualization exercise. You may use this script.**

Today we are going to be thinking about a Peaceful Place. Try to think about a place where you have felt really peaceful. It can be a real place, a place you've been to on vacation, your own backyard, or a place in your imagination.

Give them a moment to think.

Now let's travel to this peaceful place. Take a look around at your Peaceful Place. Are you inside or outside? What is the weather like? What can you see there? Are there trees? Is there water? If you are in a room, what color are the walls? Look around and really try to notice everything that you can see in your Peaceful Place.

Take another look around and see what you might have missed. **Pause.**

Now I'd like you to listen closely. What sounds do you hear in your Peaceful Place? Do you hear birds, or the sound of the waves crashing into the shore? Do you hear people talking? Music? What else do you hear? **Pause.**

What does it smell like in your Peaceful Place? Do you smell salty air? Sunscreen? Freshly cut grass? Cookies baking? What else do you smell in your Peaceful Place?

Pause.

What can you feel with your body in your Peaceful Place? Do you feel sand under your feet and between your toes? Do you feel water? Is it cold or warm? Can you feel the sun on your face? Do you feel a soft blanket? What else do you feel in your Peaceful Place?

Pause.

What does it feel like in your heart to be in your Peaceful Place? What kind of peaceful feeling do you have? Happy, safe, welcome, relaxed? Try to notice how you feel in your heart in your Peaceful Place.

Pause.

Now we are going to travel back to this peaceful place right here in our classroom.

In a moment you will hear the sound of the bells and that will mean that it is time to open your eyes. So just get ready for that.

Ask the MH to ring the bell.

Ask the MH to choose a classmate to turn the lights on.

Ask the MH to return to his or her seat.

3. Reflect and discuss

Ask some children to share a few details about their Peaceful Places.

 Kindness Pals

Do the Kindness Pals activity as before. If you don't have time for sharing, just assign the new Kindness Pals.

Closing words: *Okay, our time is up for today. Thank you for a great class, everyone. Let's have a nice quiet moment for the bell. If you want to, you can close your eyes, picture your new Kindness Pal, and imagine yourself doing something kind for them this week.*

Ring the bell.

Week 25
The THiNK Test

OBJECTIVE: Learn how to think before you speak.

Practice kindness.

PREPARE: A bell or chime

Your Kindness Pals list and Talking Object

Board or flip chart with this quote written clearly for all to read:

"Before you speak, ask yourself if what you are about to say is true, is helpful, is necessary, is kind. If the answer is no, then maybe what you are about to say should be left unsaid."

-Bernard Meltzer

 Mindfulness Practice

Invite today's Mindfulness Helper (MH) to come to the front of the class to sit next to you on a chair.

Prompt the MH to choose another student to turn off the classroom lights.

Prompt the MH to say: "Let's get into our mindful bodies. Let's close our eyes. Let's take 3 deep breaths."

Say: *Let your breath settle back into its natural rhythm. You don't have to change it at all. Let's spend a few moments counting our breaths. Remember that if your mind wanders away from your breath, don't worry about it. Just gently bring your mind back to counting your breaths.*

Give them a minute or two *to sit and quietly count. You can remind them once in a while to "notice where your mind is now."*

Say: *Now let's take one more deep breath in and out. In a moment you will hear the sound of the bell and that will mean that it is time to open your eyes.*

Ask the MH to ring the bell.

|

Ask the MH to choose a classmate to turn the lights on.

Ask the MH to return to his or her seat.

 1. **Have a few students read the quote from the board, one at a time.**

   See if they can do it from memory.

2. **Discuss**

   Ask the students what the quote means to them.

3. **Introduce the THiNK test.**

   Suggest to the students: *This is a great quote, but it's too long and hard to remember.*

   You might then **say**: *It's easier when it's broken down into the THiNK Test. This stands for:*

T:	true
H:	helpful
N:	necessary
K:	kind.

   Write THiNK on the board across in big letters and then write the words TRUE, HELPFUL, NECESSARY, KIND going down from the top under the corresponding letter.

   > NOTE: The "I" stands for "I" as in "I THINK before I speak".

4. **Talk about ways and times to use the THiNK Test.**

   Say:

   Suppose you want to tell everyone in your class that you are having a birthday party this weekend. First ask yourself, does it pass the THiNK test?

   Talk about how the answer might be different if everyone in your class is invited or only a few kids are invited.

Try it with these scenarios too:

- You want to tell someone in your class that you don't like their new haircut.
- You want to tell someone that her sneakers are out of style.

5. Role Plays

Choose four kids to represent the different words: Mr. True, Ms. Helpful, Mr. Necessary and Ms. Kind.

Ask them to try to answer these and similar questions.

Repeat with a new group of four students.

- You want to tell someone in your choir that their voice is bad.
- You want to tell everyone that you got an A on the test.
- You want to tell someone that you just heard that "Ellen" likes "Fred."
- You want to tell someone that the TV show they like is for babies.
- You want to tell your class that it is your birthday (talk about when that would be appropriate—during a test? During a lesson? At recess? At morning meeting?).
- You want to tell your parents that your friend is getting bullied, but your friend told you not to tell anyone.
- You want to tell someone that his zipper is unzipped.
- Someone is spreading a rumor that you like "Ernie" and you want to set the record straight that you don't like him (again a question of time, place, etc.).

Ask for more examples or take their questions.

 Kindness Pals

Do the Kindness Pals activity as before. If you don't have time for sharing, just assign the new Kindness Pals.

Closing words: *Okay, our time is up for today. Thank you for a great class, everyone. Let's have a nice quiet moment for the bell. If you want to, you can close your eyes, picture your new Kindness Pal, and imagine yourself doing something kind for them this week.*

Ring the bell.

Week 26
Kindness Chain

OBJECTIVES: Show the power of our words and to illustrate how
one act of kindness can set off a chain of kindness.
Practice kindness.

PREPARE: A bell or chime
Your Kindness Pals list and Talking Object.

 Mindfulness Practice

Invite today's Mindfulness Helper (MH) to come to the front of the class to sit next to you on a chair.

Prompt the MH to choose another student to turn off the classroom lights.

Prompt the MH to say: "Let's get into our mindful bodies. Let's close our eyes. Let's take 3 deep breaths."

Say: *Let your breath settle back into its natural rhythm. You don't have to change it at all. Let's spend a few moments counting our breaths. Remember that if your mind wanders away from your breath, don't worry about it. Just gently bring your mind back to counting your breaths.*

Give them a minute or two *to sit and quietly count. You can remind them once in a while to "notice where your mind is now."*

Say: *Now let's take one more deep breath in and out. In a moment you will hear the sound of the bell and that will mean that it is time to open your eyes.*

Ask the MH to ring the bell.

Ask the MH to choose a classmate to turn the lights on.

Ask the MH to return to his or her seat.

1. **Write on the board: "Words are like toothpaste."**

   Ask the kids to comment on what they think that means.

2. **Introduce the Lesson**

   You might say:

   When I say "words are like toothpaste," I am thinking about how once you squeeze the toothpaste out of the tube, it is impossible to put it back in.

   The same is true for our words.

   Once you say something to someone, it is out there. Even if you really regret it or didn't really mean it, it's still out there. There is no way to put the words back in your mouth and make them disappear. That is why it's so important to think about our words before we say them and to recognize that our words have power.

   Words are so powerful that with our words we can make someone feel wonderful. For example, I might say to my friend, "Wow, you are such an amazing artist! You should enter a competition."

   My friend might respond in a positive way, and my words might give her the confidence to enter that contest and continue to make her art.

   But what might happen if I say to my friend, "Uh, that drawing doesn't look anything like a horse. Maybe you should stick to baseball." What do you think might happen?

   Pause for some comments.

   So maybe my friend will say "Well, that's your opinion, but I love drawing and I'm going to keep trying."

   Or maybe my friend will feel embarrassed and awful and will crumple up her paper and never draw again.

   Our words have a lot of power. So it's important to think about what we say. Over the next few lessons, we are going to be thinking about our words in a few different ways. Today we are going to be using our words to make people feel good.

Today we are going to make a Kindness Chain.

3. Describe the Kindness Chain Exercise

We are going to go around the circle, and I'd like you to say something kind about the person sitting to your right. For example, I might say: "Cheryl, you are an awesome friend."

Cheryl might say "Thanks!" and then turn to the person on her right and say, "Harry, you are really good at building things."

And we'll go around the circle like that. Every once in a while when we play this game somebody's mind goes blank, and they can't think of anything to say. Even if they are sitting next to their best friend! If that happens to you, don't worry. Just say "I need some help." I will choose a volunteer to say something kind about that person and then we'll continue going around the circle.

When we're done we'll go around the circle in the other direction.

This is a chance to use the power of our words to make people feel really good, so let's try hard to take it seriously and make sure that everybody feels good. Ready to start?"

4. Reflect and Discuss

Ask the children to share what it felt like to give and receive these compliments and what it feels like to use the power of your words for good.

 Kindness Pals

Do the Kindness Pals activity as before. If you don't have time for sharing, just assign the new Kindness Pals.

Closing words: *Okay, our time is up for today. Thank you for a great class, everyone. Let's have a nice quiet moment for the bell. If you want to, you can close your eyes, picture your new Kindness Pal, and imagine yourself doing something kind for them this week.*

Ring the bell.

Week 27
Exclusion

OBJECTIVES: Raise awareness of the effect of leaving people out.

Practice kindness.

PREPARE: A bell or chime

Copies of the *Exclusion on the Playground* Skit found in Resource Section

Your Kindness Pals list and Talking Object

 Mindfulness Practice

Invite today's Mindfulness Helper (MH) to come to the front of the class to sit next to you on a chair.

Prompt the MH to choose another student to turn off the classroom lights.

Prompt the MH to say: "Let's get into our mindful bodies. Let's close our eyes. Let's take 3 deep breaths."

Say: *Let your breath settle back into its natural rhythm. You don't have to change it at all. Let's spend a few moments counting our breaths. Remember that if your mind wanders away from your breath, don't worry about it. Just gently bring your mind back to counting your breaths.*

Give them a minute or two *to sit and quietly count. You can remind them once in a while to "notice where your mind is now."*

Say: *Now let's take one more deep breath in and out. In a moment you will hear the sound of the bell and that will mean that it is time to open your eyes.*

Ask the MH to ring the bell.

Ask the MH to choose a classmate to turn the lights on.

Ask the MH to return to his or her seat.

1. **Introduce the Lesson**

   You might say:

   Today we are going to do a skit. This skit is about what happens when a new kid is being left out at school. Three other kids are talking about him. One child is trying to get them to include him by helping them see things from his perspective and relate to him. Once they can see things from his point of view, they decide to include him.

2. **Assign parts** to 7 students. If you have a different mix of boys/girls just change the character names accordingly.

3. **Have your first** cast act out the skit.

4. **Re-assign parts** and have your second cast act out the skit.

5. **Discuss. You might ask:**

   - Why were the kids excluding the new kid?

   - What convinced them to ask him to join them?

   - Have you ever been excluded? How did it feel? What were the circumstances?

   - Have you ever excluded someone? Did you realize that you were doing it? Did you think about the feelings of the person being excluded?

   - Why do you think kids are more likely to get bullied when they are being excluded?

   - What did it feel like to play the different parts? The kid being excluded, the kids doing the excluding, the kid standing up for the new kid?

 Kindness Pals

   Do the Kindness Pals activity as before. If you don't have time for sharing, just assign the new Kindness Pals.

   Closing words: *Okay, our time is up for today. Thank you for a great class, everyone. Let's have a nice quiet moment for the bell. If you want to, you can close your eyes, picture your new Kindness Pal, and imagine yourself doing something kind for them this week.*

   Ring the bell.

Fun with Mindfulness

OBJECTIVES: Have fun learning about Mindfulness.

Practice kindness.

PREPARE: A bell or chime

A means to show YouTube videos to your class.

The link to *Don't Flip Yo Lid* by JusTme, performed by the students of Glenview Elementary School, Madison WI. https://www.youtube.com/watch?v=he-fW9_3egw

Your Kindness Pals list and Talking Object

 Mindfulness Practice

Invite today's Mindfulness Helper (MH) to come to the front of the class to sit next to you on a chair.

Prompt the MH to choose another student to turn off the classroom lights.

Prompt the MH to say: "Let's get into our mindful bodies. Let's close our eyes. Let's take 3 deep breaths."

Say: *Let your breath settle back into its natural rhythm. You don't have to change it at all. Let's spend a few moments counting our breaths. Remember that if your mind wanders away from your breath, don't worry about it. Just gently bring your mind back to counting your breaths.*

Give them a minute or two *to sit and quietly count. You can remind them once in a while to "notice where your mind is now."*

Say: *Now let's take one more deep breath in and out. In a moment you will hear the sound of the bell and that will mean that it is time to open your eyes.*

Ask the MH to ring the bell.

Ask the MH to choose a classmate to turn the lights on.

Ask the MH to return to his or her seat.

1. **Review** what students learned about their brains in previous lessons.

2. **Introduce JustMe,** a rapper who teaches mindfulness. He has written new words to songs to teach children about mindfulness.

3. **Play *Don't Flip Yo Lid*** for the class.

4. **Have children raise their hands** when they hear some of the parts of the brain that they have learned about.

5. **The Counting Game**

   This is a fun Mindfulness game that is sometimes used in theater classes. It works here nicely because it teaches the children to listen mindfully, to focus completely on a task, to be patient with one another, and to work together as a team.

   Start out with the kids sitting close together if possible. Tell everyone that they are going to try to count to ten as a group.

   You might use this script to introduce the game and provide guidance:

   Today we are going to try to count to ten as a group. That sounds easy but it's actually pretty hard.

   We are going to close our eyes and listen carefully.

   At some point one of you will say "one" and then someone else will say "two" and we'll keep going until we get to ten.

   The challenge is that every time I hear two of you say a number at the same time you'll have to start all over again.

   To make the game work, you are going to have to listen very carefully to each other.

   You are also going to have to be mindful of not taking too many turns.

   You also have to be mindful of making sure that you participate.

   If we get to ten, we can keep going.

To start things out, I will say, "Start and go." Every time I hear two of you say a number at the same time I will say, "Start again and go."

Please don't make a lot of noise when that happens. Just take a deep breath and start over again. Ready to try it?

> NOTE: *This game is harder than it sounds. Encourage the children to be patient and kind with each other. There will of course be kids who want to say all the numbers who might need gentle reminders not to dominate the game, and there will also be those too afraid to chime in who will need encouragement. My students love this game and want to play it every time we meet.*

Kindness Pals

Do the Kindness Pals activity as before. If you don't have time for sharing, just assign the new Kindness Pals.

Closing words: *Okay, our time is up for today. Thank you for a great class, everyone. Let's have a nice quiet moment for the bell. If you want to, you can close your eyes, picture your new Kindness Pal, and imagine yourself doing something kind for them this week.*

Ring the bell.

Week 29
Say Something – Part 1

OBJECTIVES: Think about what it feels like to be teased or bullied.

                          Practice kindness.

PREPARE: A bell or chime

                          Say Something by Peggy Moss

                          Your Kindness Pals list and Talking Object

 Mindfulness Practice

Invite today's Mindfulness Helper (MH) to come to the front of the class to sit next to you on a chair.

Prompt the MH to choose another student to turn off the classroom lights.

Prompt the MH to say: "Let's get into our mindful bodies. Let's close our eyes. Let's take 3 deep breaths."

Say: *I'm going to describe a few different situations and I'd like you to imagine that they are happening to you. Try to notice how you feel and where in your body you feel it.*

- Imagine that you are playing with a few kids at recess, and somebody runs up and says something mean to your friend. Everybody except your friend laughs at what he says, including you. How do you feel? Where do you feel it?

- Now imagine that you are playing with a few kids at recess, and somebody runs up and says something mean to your friend. The other kids laugh, but you don't. You walk over to your friend and say "Let's get out of here." How do you feel? Where do you feel it?

- Imagine that you are playing with a few kids at recess and somebody runs up and says something mean to you. Everybody laughs except for you. How do you feel? Where do you feel it?

- Now imagine that you are playing with a few kids at recess and somebody runs up and says something mean to you. Everybody laughs except for one person. She comes over to you and says, "Let's get out of here." How do you feel? Where do you feel it?

- Imagine you are outside at recess and you run up to some kids and you say something mean to one of them. Everybody laughs except for the person you were mean to. How do you feel? Where do you feel it?

- Imagine you are outside at recess and you run up to some kids and you say something mean to one of them. Nobody laughs. How do you feel? Where do you feel it?

Say: *Let's all take another nice deep breath. Let's listen for the sound of the breathing bells. When you hear the bell, it will be time to open your eyes.*

Ask the MH to ring the bell when the mindful breathing is complete.

Ask the MH to choose a classmate to turn the lights on.

Ask the MH to return to his or her seat.

Ring the Bell.

Give students time to share how they were feeling in each scenario.

 1. **Read** the story to the class.

This is a book about a girl who watches other kids at her school get teased and bullied. She doesn't say anything until she herself becomes a target. This is a powerful story that usually has a sobering effect on students of this age.

2. **Discuss.** You might ask:

- Have you ever wanted to say something to help someone but were afraid or unsure of what to say?
- Why don't people speak up when they see someone being mistreated?
- Do you have to say something with words to help?
- How could you help with your actions?

3. **Suggest:**

You could stand next to the person being teased or sit next to them like the storyteller did in Say Something.

You could play with someone who is being teased or quickly walk them to somewhere safer.

 Kindness Pals

Do the Kindness Pals activity as before. If you don't have time for sharing, just assign the new Kindness Pals.

Closing words: *Okay, our time is up for today. Thank you for a great class, everyone. Let's have a nice quiet moment for the bell. If you want to, you can close your eyes, picture your new Kindness Pal, and imagine yourself doing something kind for them this week.*

Ring the bell.

Say Something – Part 2

OBJECTIVES: Apply the lessons from the book <u>Say Something</u> to daily life.

Practice kindness.

PREPARE: A bell or chime

Copies of *Say Something* skits from Resource Section

Your Kindness Pals list and Talking Object

 Mindfulness Practice

Invite today's Mindfulness Helper (MH) to come to the front of the class to sit next to you on a chair.

Prompt the MH to choose another student to turn off the classroom lights.

Prompt the MH to say: "Let's get into our mindful bodies. Let's close our eyes. Let's take 3 deep breaths."

Say: *Let your breath settle back into its natural rhythm. You don't have to change it at all. Let's spend a few moments counting our breaths. Remember that if your mind wanders away from your breath, don't worry about it. Just gently bring your mind back to counting your breaths.*

Give them a minute or two *to sit and quietly count. You can remind them once in a while to "notice where your mind is now."*

Say: *Now let's take one more deep breath in and out. In a moment you will hear the sound of the bell and that will mean that it is time to open your eyes.*

Ask the MH to ring the bell.

Ask the MH to choose a classmate to turn the lights on.

Ask the MH to return to his or her seat.

1. Say Something Skits

Introduce the *Say Something* skits. Tell the class they are about kids like them who are in a difficult position.

Hand out copies of the *Say Something* Skits.

Choose five volunteers to act out the skit.

Invite the actors to present the skit to the class.

Read the stage directions in italics for the actors.

2. Discussion

Ask, after the skit:

- How do you think Sammy felt about the way Crystal and her friends were treating him?
- Was his friend Mackie trying to help him?
- Did someone finally say something to Crystal?
- Did Crystal listen when her friends asked her to stop bothering Sammy?
- What finally convinced Crystal to stop?
- Do you think it was hard for Luis and Jei to stand up to Crystal?
- Would it be hard for you to tell a friend that they were being mean to someone?
- Did going over to sit with Mackie and Sammy "say something" to Crystal?
- What did it say?
- What did it say to Sammy?

3. Reflection and Action

Share these thoughts with the class:

Sometimes our actions can speak very loudly. If we feel like someone is being treated badly, it isn't enough to feel sorry for him or her. We have to try to help.

There are lots of different ways to help when someone is being teased.

We can say something to the person being teased, like "are you okay?" or "do you want to come and sit with me?"

We can say something to the person doing the teasing, like "Hey, that's not funny." or "Come on, give it a rest." Or even just "Dude."

We can say something with our actions like the boys in this skit and the girl in <u>Say Something</u>. Just going over and standing next to someone being teased or mistreated (as long as you are physically safe) can be really powerful.

People tend to pick on kids who are often alone so standing next to them can be a powerful deterrent. You don't have to make a big speech to make an impact.

Think about what you can do and then, do it!

Kindness Pals

Do the Kindness Pals activity as before. If you don't have time for sharing, just assign the new Kindness Pals.

Closing words: *Okay, our time is up for today. Thank you for a great class, everyone. Let's have a nice quiet moment for the bell. If you want to, you can close your eyes, picture your new Kindness Pal, and imagine yourself doing something kind for them this week.*

Ring the bell.

Week 31
Mindful Eating

OBJECTIVES: Apply our Mindfulness skills to our everyday lives.

Practice kindness.

PREPARE: A bell or chime

Enough raisins for all of your class to have one or two

<u>No Ordinary Apple</u> by Sara Marlowe

Your Kindness Pals list and Talking Objects

 Mindfulness Practice

Invite today's Mindfulness Helper (MH) to come to the front of the class to sit next to you on a chair.

Prompt the MH to choose another student to turn off the classroom lights.

Prompt the MH to say: "Let's get into our mindful bodies. Let's close our eyes. Let's take 3 deep breaths."

Say: *Let your breath settle back into its natural rhythm. You don't have to change it at all. Let's spend a few moments counting our breaths. Remember that if your mind wanders away from your breath, don't worry about it. Just gently bring your mind back to counting your breaths.*

Give them a minute or two *to sit and quietly count. You can remind them once in a while to "notice where your mind is now."*

Say: *Now let's take one more deep breath in and out. In a moment you will hear the sound of the bell and that will mean that it is time to open your eyes.*

Ask the MH to ring the bell.

Ask the MH to choose a classmate to turn the lights on.

Ask the MH to return to his or her seat.

1. **Read the book, <u>No Ordinary Apple</u>.**

   This is a story about a little boy who discovers that eating something as ordinary as an apple can become a wonderful experience when he eats it mindfully using all of his senses.

2. **Introduce and lead the Mindful Eating exercise. You might say:**

   Now we are going to see what it feels like to eat something mindfully.

   I am going to give you each one raisin. I'd like you to put your hand out in front of you. Please wait for me to bring you your raisin.

   When you get your raisin just let it sit there on your open hand, please don't touch it or move it until I ask you to.

   If you think you don't like raisins, don't worry. We are going to do a lot of different things with the raisin and you don't have to eat it if you don't want to.

   Place a raisin in each child's hand.

   Now that everyone has his or her raisin, I'd like you to you take a look at yours. Don't touch it. Just use your eyes and see what you notice about your raisin. Who would like to share what they see?

   Take a few responses.

   Now I'd like to notice how your raisin smells? What do you notice? Try smelling your raisin with your eyes closed and then with your eyes open. Do you notice any difference?

   Encourage the children not to get too focused on whether or not they like the raisin. Encourage them to notice the raisin without judgment.

   Now let's bring our attention to how our raisin feels. Take your finger and gently touch your raisin. What do you notice?

   Now this might sound funny, but I'd like you to notice what your raisin sounds like. Pick it up with your fingers and put it next to your ear. If you wiggle it back and forth a little with your fingers you might notice a sound. What do you notice?

Now listen very carefully to these instructions.

Place your raisin right in the middle of your tongue and keep your mouth open.

Raise your hand if you can taste your raisin.

Try moving the raisin with your fingers to different places on your tongue and notice if your raisin tastes different in different parts of your tongue.

Now very gently take a bite of your raisin. Notice what happens. Does your raisin taste different than it did before you bit into it? Now you can chew your raisin. Notice what it feels like when you swallow it. See how long you can feel it going down.

3. Reflect and Discuss

Use these questions to help the class reflect on their experience.

- What did it feel like to eat mindfully?
- Is this the way you usually eat?
- Can you imagine yourself eating your dinner mindfully tonight?

You might conclude with: *Your assignment today is try to eat one thing mindfully today. Enjoy!*

 Kindness Pals

Do the Kindness Pals activity as before. If you don't have time for sharing, just assign the new Kindness Pals.

Closing words: *Okay, our time is up for today. Thank you for a great class, everyone. Let's have a nice quiet moment for the bell. If you want to, you can close your eyes, picture your new Kindness Pal, and imagine yourself doing something kind for them this week.*

Ring the bell.

Week 32
Kindest Things

OBJECTIVES: Encourage the children to see the good in each other and experience the good feeling of sharing heartfelt compliments.

PREPARE: Paper, pen or pencil for every student in the class.

> NOTE FROM LINDA *This is a wonderful activity that has been very meaningful to my students over the years. It is a bit time-consuming for the teacher because you are going to be typing up a page for each child that lists all of the kind things the class said about him or her. I hope that you will do it anyway.*
>
> *I have found that I learn more about my students from what they say about other people than from what others say about them. I have had many students tell me that they have kept their Kindest Things page on their walls all the way through college! It's worth the work. I've done it for up to 100 kids every year and it is time well-spent.*

😌 Mindfulness Practice

Invite today's Mindfulness Helper (MH) to come to the front of the class to sit next to you on a chair.

Prompt the MH to choose another student to turn off the classroom lights.

Prompt the MH to say: "Let's get into our mindful bodies. Let's close our eyes. Let's take 3 deep breaths."

Check to see that all students are sitting comfortably with their eyes closed or looking down.

Say: *I'd like you to think about someone who makes you happy. Choose someone you see every day at home or at school. You might choose someone in your family, a friend, a teacher, even a pet. Just choose someone and try to picture that person happy and smiling. Picture them doing something that makes them happy. Try to notice how you feel when you think about this person.*

Now, if you'd like to, fill your heart up with kindness and repeat these words in your mind while you think about this person:

May you be happy. **Wait a moment.**

May you be healthy. **Wait a moment.**

May you be peaceful. **Wait a moment.**

Take a moment to notice how you feel. Any way that you feel is fine, even if you feel nothing. Just try to notice it.

Invite the students to share whom they were thinking about.

Now take a deep breath, and listen for the sound of the bell. When you hear that sound it will be time to open your eyes.

Ask the MH to ring the bell when the mindful breathing is complete.

Ask the MH to choose a classmate to turn the lights back on.

Ask the MH to return to his or her seat.

 1. Read these instructions aloud.

These instructions are long, but it's really important that the kids get the sense of reverence in this activity.

Today we are going to do something very powerful. We have talked about how we can use our words to hurt or to help others. Today we are going to use our words to be kind to each other.

I am going to ask you to think about the kindest thing you can think of to say about each person in the class.

We are going to go one by one. I will say the name of someone in the class and write that person's name on the board. You will write down one or two things about that person.

*You might think about what is special about that person—a talent they have, a time when they were kind to you, maybe they are always friendly to new people, maybe they always make you laugh, maybe you admire them for being brave, or creative or artistic, etc. Do **not** just use the first thing that pops into your head.*

You will write your name on your paper, but only I will see it. Each comment will be anonymous.

IMPORTANT: there will be absolutely no talking during this exercise. We are holding each person in the class in our kindness circle. Giggling or talking can sometimes lead to accidental unkindness or misunderstandings. Anyone who cannot abide by the rule of silence will be asked to wait in the hall and will not participate.

After class I will type up a paper for each one of you with all of the kind things your classmates said about you. You won't be able to see who said what, but you will see what they said. This will take me a while, but I will return them to you soon. Make sure that you share your paper with your family!

2. Lead the Class through the Exercise

Write the first student's name on the board so everyone can see the spelling.

Say: *"Now we will think about (Name). What is the kindest thing you can think of to say about (Name)? What is special about (Name)?"*

Give a minute or more for each child depending on how much time you have.

When the exercise is over, give them time to catch up on anybody they missed and then collect the papers.

3. Ask the class to share what this experience was like for them.

♡ Kindness Pals

Do Kindness Pals as before, but do not give out new pals.

Closing words: *This is our last class together, so I will not be handing out new kindness pals today.*

I hope that you enjoyed learning more about mindfulness, and kindness, and how to work out our conflicts peacefully. The world needs lots of kind, mindful people. Now you have some tools to help you go out into the world and make it a more peaceful place. I hope you will!

Mr. Gregal's Fifth Grade Class
Said the Kindest Things About:
Izara

Enthusiastic; makes friends easily;
always fun and stylish; funny and athletic;
awesome, smart, kind, caring, funny, friendly,
generous, playful, & supportive;
good helper;
beautiful, funny, kind, has a lot of energy, funny;
enthusiastic; good singer and awesome at dancing;
kind and enthusiastic; kind; you're a great dancer;
always knows what to say; smart;
funny; funny, kind, friendly;
selfless and brave; kind;
fun, friendly, organized;
funny and a good singer;
kind and generous;
fun to be around, hyper in a good way;
Izara is kind.

Ms. Ryden's Peace Class 2015

Resources

I think Peace class is important because it helps soothe your brain and if you have any problems Peace class will help you figure it out. Also it helps bring your mind back to what you were working on.

— Peace of Mind Student

Program Extensions

Consider moving the lessons of **Peace of Mind** beyond the classroom with one or more of these Program extensions. Each offers opportunities for students to hone their new mindfulness skills, to practice kindness, and to use the common language and tools they are learning to resolve conflicts.

Daily Mindful Moments

The **Peace of Mind** curriculum is designed to be used in a weekly class. If you have the time and desire to make **Peace of Mind** a part of your classroom every day, we salute you! Daily Mindful Moments are a great way for your students to practice the skills that they are learning weekly in **Peace of Mind** class and to enjoy a moment of calm and quiet before beginning a new activity. It just takes a couple of minutes. Once you get into the habit that it will be something that is beneficial to both you and your students.

You may want to make "Mindfulness Helper" a weekly job in your classroom and have that student lead the Daily Mindful Moment. You may decide to lead the Daily Mindful Moment yourself at the beginning to set the tone and expectations and then transition to a student-led practice. Either way is fine. You can also experiment with the duration of the quiet moment. Some classes will have no problem with two minutes and will quickly graduate to more; some classes will be better off with one minute or less to start. Refer to Week 16 for a short mindfulness practice to follow, including the Mindfulness Helper.

Peace Club

Peace Club is a lunch and recess program for students who need a smaller alternative to the cafeteria and the playground. It can be a mixed-age group of anywhere from 20-50 students. Peace Club is meant to be a comfortable option for kids who sometimes struggle with their social skills or with being in a large group. It is also popular among kids who like to make a difference and who make a commitment to making everyone feel welcome and respected.

At Lafayette Elementary School, for example, children on the autism spectrum and with other diagnoses often have Peace Club specifically written into their IEP's and 504 plans because Peace Club provides some structured play as well as informal group counseling during the hour.

Peace Club requires all students who come to make a promise to treat everyone else with kindness and respect and to make sure that conflicts are worked out peacefully and everyone is included. Fourth and fifth graders might serve as special helpers. These are kids who make an extra commitment to seek out those who have a harder time jumping in and include them in games, and who help others work out conflicts peacefully.

Peace Heroes

Peace Heroes is a way to recognize children who make an extra effort to be kind. One way to do this is to have a box somewhere in the school where kids or adults can write a note recognizing another student for an act of kindness. The names can be posted on a bulletin board somewhere in the school. Once a month some of the names can be read on school-wide announcements.

Linkages to Behavior Management Programs

The concepts underlying the **Peace of Mind** program can be adapted to work with classroom management programs like Positive Behavioral Intervention and Supports (PBIS) or Responsive Classroom. School-wide expectations can be expressed in "mindful" language—for example: "Speak Mindfully, Act Mindfully, Move Mindfully." Most of the things that we are expecting the children to do at school fall into these three categories. Children can be encouraged to "move mindfully" in the hallways, instead of saying "No running!" or to "speak mindfully" instead of "don't blurt out," or to "act mindfully" instead of "be responsible." This subtle shift in language can help children understand the reasons for our rules and make them more likely to follow them.

Skits for this Curriculum

All of the skits included in this curriculum are original works by Linda Ryden, written specifically for the **Peace of Mind** curriculum.

In this section you will find the skits referenced in the curriculum that you may copy and hand out to your students.

1. Week 12: Rosie's Brain Skit

2. Week 17, 21: Conflict Resolution: Scrabble vs. Monopoly Skits 1

3. Week 17: Conflict Resolution: Scrabble vs. Monopoly Skit 2

4. Week 18: Conflict Resolution: Class Party Skit 1

5. Week 18: Conflict Resolution: Class Party Skit 2

6. Week 27: Exclusion on the Playground Skit

7. Week 30: Say Something Skit

Week 12 Skit
Rosie's Brain

By Linda Ryden

Topic:	Understanding our brains
Characters:	Rosie's Mom, Rosie, Sophie, Amygdala, Hippocampus, Prefrontal Cortex (PFC)
Setting:	Rosie's home and school

Rosie's Mom: Rosie, remember, you have a piano lesson after school today.

Rosie: Okay!

Rosie's Mom: Don't forget!

Later that day at school:

Sophie: Hey Rosie, do you want to come over after school today?

Rosie: Hmmm… (*looks like she's thinking and reacting to what her brain is saying*)

Amygdala: Oh my gosh! That's so exciting! I love playing with Sophie! Yay yay yay!!!!!!!!!!!!!!!!!!

Hippocampus: Oh Rosie…. Don't you remember that you have a piano lesson after school today?

Amygdala: Oh nooooo! That's the worst news ever!!! I'm devastated. I'm going to throw a total tantrum right here, right now!

PFC: Hang on now Amygdala. Are you sure that's the best idea? Maybe we can come up with a solution to this problem.

Amygdala: No, there is no solution! It's a disaster, it's the worst thing that has ever happened (*breathing hard*).

PFC: Now, now, don't flip your lid. Why don't you do your mindful breathing?

Hippocampus: Oh I remember that! We learned about it in Peace Class. It's when you breathe in and out to help you to calm down.

PFC: That's right. Let's give it a try.

Rosie: (*Starts taking deep breaths in and out.*)

Amygdala: Hey, I'm starting to feel better. Maybe this isn't the worst problem ever.

Hippocampus: You know, I remember other times when throwing tantrums didn't turn out very well and made things worse.

PFC: Me too. Now that you've calmed down, Amygdala, I think I have come up with a solution to the problem. Why don't we get together with Sophie after your piano lesson?

Amygdala: That's a great idea! Thanks PFC!

Hippocampus: Remember the last time you had a playdate with Sophie and you ate pizza together?

Amygdala: That's right! Maybe we can do that again today.

PFC: Why don't we ask her?

Rosie: Hey Sophie, I have a piano lesson after school so can we have our play-date afterwards and maybe eat some pizza?

Sophie: Sounds great!!

All: Yay!!

Weeks 17 and 21
Skit: Scrabble vs. Monopoly 1

By Linda Ryden

Topic: Conflict Resolution

Characters: Charlie, Henry, Julio, Lucy, Reign, Alice

Scene: Charlie's house. The kids are having a playdate.

Charlie: Hey guys, let's play Monopoly! I just got a new game and I've been dying to play it.

Henry: That sounds great! I love Monopoly!

Julio: Yes! Monopoly is my favorite game!

Lucy: No way! Monopoly takes too long to play. Let's play Scrabble instead!

Reign: Yeah, Scrabble is awesome. I'm really good!

Alice: That's because you're a really good speller.

Reign: Thanks!

Charlie: What are you guys talking about? Monopoly is the coolest game. Scrabble is for geeks.

Lucy: Who are you calling a geek? You're a loser.

Henry: Yeah, Scrabble is boring. Only boring people like to play Scrabble.

Reign: If you guys are going to play Monopoly then Lucy and Alice and I are leaving!

Charlie: Fine with me! We don't like playing with dumb girls anyway!

Lucy, **Reign**, and **Alice** storm out.

Week 17 Skit
Scrabble vs. Monopoly 2

By Linda Ryden

Topic:	**Conflict Resolution**
Characters:	**Charlie, Henry, Julio, Lucy, Reign, Alice**
Scene:	**Charlie's house. The kids are having a playdate**

Charlie: Hey guys, let's play Monopoly*!* I just got a new game and I've been dying to play it.

Henry: That sounds great! I love Monopoly!

Julio: Yes! Monopoly is my favorite game!

Lucy: No way! Monopoly takes too long to play. Let's play Scrabble instead!

Reign: Yeah, Scrabble is awesome. I'm really good!

Alice: That's because you're a really good speller.

Reign: Thanks!

Charlie: What are you talking about? Monopoly is the coolest game. Scrabble is for geeks!

Lucy: Who are you calling a geek? You're a loser.

Henry: Hey you guys, we're going up the Conflict Escalator.

Reign: Oh, you're right. There's nothing but trouble at the top of the Conflict Escalator!

Julio: Why don't we calm down a bit? Let's take some deep breaths.

Everybody stops and takes three deep breaths.

Lucy: Hey, Charlie, I'm sorry I called you a loser. I didn't mean it.

Charlie: No, I'm sorry. I shouldn't have said Scrabble is for geeks. I like Scrabble. I was just really excited to play Monopoly and I got carried away.

Alice: I have an idea! Why don't we take turns. We can play Monopoly today and then tomorrow we can go over to my house and play Scrabble.

All: That's a great idea!

Peace of
Mind

Week 18 Skit
The Class Party 1

By Linda Ryden

Topic:	**Conflict Resolution**
Characters:	**Richard Leslie, Carlos, Diana, Oscar**
Scene:	**Classroom during indoor recess.**

Richard: I'm so excited about this party!

Oscar: Yeah, me too. I can't believe the teacher is letting us come up with the theme.

Carlos: I know, it's going to be awesome! I think we should have a chocolate theme. We could fill the entire classroom with chocolate and just swim around in it for the whole day!

All: Carlos!

Diana: Carlos, that is a ridiculous idea. Although it does sound like fun. We have to come up with something the teacher will actually let us do.

Leslie: How about a craft party? We could set up lots of stations and make a bunch of different crafts.

Richard: Nah, that sounds boring. All you ever want to do is make little crafty things. I think we should have a Star Wars theme.

Oscar: Yeah, we could have huge light saber fights!

Carlos: Cool! And the light sabers could be made of chocolate.

All: Carlos!

Diana: Not everybody likes Star Wars and the fighting sounds too violent. How about a Harry Potter party?

Leslie: I love Harry Potter!

Oscar: Harry Potter is stupid—I hate all that magic stuff.

Diana: Harry Potter isn't stupid. You're stupid!

Richard: We're never going to agree on a party theme. You girls have such dumb girlie ideas. I wouldn't come to any party that you planned.

Oscar: Me neither.

Diana: Well, fine. I wouldn't come to your stinky party either. Maybe the teacher will let us have separate parties.

Leslie: That would be great—that way we don't have to talk to you anymore.

Richard and **Oscar** and **Carlos**: Fine with us!

Everyone storms out.

Peace of
Mind

Week 18 Skit
The Class Party 2

By Linda Ryden

Topic:	**Conflict Resolution**
Characters:	**Richard, Leslie, Carlos, Diana, Oscar**
Scene:	**Classroom during indoor recess.**

Richard: I'm so excited about this party!

Oscar: Yeah, me too. I can't believe the teacher is letting us come up with the theme.

Carlos: I know, it's going to be awesome! I think we should have a chocolate theme. We could fill the entire classroom with chocolate and just swim around in it for the whole day!

All: Carlos!

Diana: Carlos, that is a ridiculous idea. Although it does sound like fun. We have to come up with something the teacher will actually let us do.

Leslie: How about a craft party? We could set up lots of stations and make a bunch of different crafts.

Richard: Nah, that sounds boring. All you ever want to do is make little crafty things. I think we should have a Star Wars theme.

Oscar: Yeah, we could have huge light saber fights!

Carlos: Cool! And the light sabers could be made of chocolate.

All: Carlos!

Diana: Not everybody likes Star Wars and the fighting sounds too violent. How about a Harry Potter party?

Leslie: I love Harry Potter!

Oscar: Harry Potter is stupid—I hate all that magic stuff.

Diana: Harry Potter isn't stupid. You're stupid!

Leslie: Hang on, we're going up the Conflict Escalator! If we keep fighting we're never going to come up with an idea and we might not get to have the party.

Richard: She's right. We need to calm down. Let's take some deep breaths.

Everybody takes three slow deep breaths.

Diana: I'm sorry I said you are stupid, Oscar. I really didn't mean it. I was just flipping my lid.

Oscar: I'm sorry too. Harry Potter isn't stupid.

Richard: And I'm sorry I said that a craft party would be boring. That was mean. I actually like making stuff, I just didn't want the whole party to be crafts.

Leslie: That's okay.

Carlos: How about having a "Go Green" party? We all care about the environment. We could make posters to put up around the school reminding people to recycle and stuff.

Diana: And we could make birdfeeders out of pine cones and peanut butter and birdseed.

Richard: Cool! And we could even make light sabers out of recycled paper towel rolls.

Carlos: And we could have a dunk tank filled with chocolate!

All: Carlos!!!

Everybody high fives each other.

Peace of Mind

Week 26 Skit
Exclusion on the Playground

By Linda Ryden

Topic:	Kindness, Inclusion
Characters:	Jason, Susan, Beth, Jerry, Mark
Setting:	Recess on playground.
	4 friends are playing together and 1 new kid is sitting alone.

Jason: Boy, I'm so glad it stopped raining! I hate indoor recess.

Susan: Me too! It's so hot in the school today.

Beth: What do you want to do? Play basketball?

Jason: Sure.

Jerry: (*looking over at Mark*) Hey, have you guys noticed that the new kid is always alone at recess?

Jason: Who cares? He's not our friend.

Susan: Yeah, we've got enough friends. He should make his own friends.

Beth: I heard that he's weird. I heard that he never talks to anyone.

Jerry: Well, he looks pretty sad and lonely. I remember when I was new at school. It was pretty scary. Nobody talked to me for a whole week.

Jason: Well, if you care so much about him, why don't you go over and play with him?

Susan: Yeah, just don't bring him over here! I don't want to play with that new kid.

Beth: Me neither. Let's go play.

Jerry: Come on, you guys! You know that it's mean to leave people out. Sometimes when people get left out all of the time they might get bullied.

Jason: You're right. When my brother was little he was always by himself because the other kids wouldn't play with him. Then a big kid started picking on him.

Beth: Gee, that's awful.

Susan: Maybe we should go over and ask him if he wants to play with us.

Beth: But he's just going to say no.

Jason: Yeah, he doesn't want to talk to anyone. He probably wants to be alone.

Susan: I don't think anyone really wants to be alone. Let's go over and try.

All: Okay.

Jason: Hi. I'm Jason. Do you want to play basketball with us?

Mark: Um, no thanks.

Jerry: Come on, it will be fun! Do you know how to play basketball?

Mark: Sure! At my old school I was on the basketball team. We won a championship.

Beth: Wow! I want you on my team!

Jason: No, be on my team!

Susan: We'll just flip a coin, okay?

Mark: Okay. Thanks!

Jerry: Come on you guys, let's go play.

All walk off happily.

Peace of
Mind

Week 30 Skit
Say Something

By Linda Ryden

Topic:	Standing up against bullying
Characters:	Sammy, Mackie, Jei, Crystal, Luis
Scene:	Cafeteria. Third graders Mackie and Sammy are eating lunch in the cafeteria at the peanut-free table.

Sammy: That concert we heard today was really cool!

Mackie: Yeah, I thought the middle school choir was awesome.

Sammy: Thanks for sitting with me.

Mackie: No problem. It's weird that there's nobody else at the peanut-free table today.

Sammy: Oh no! Here comes Crystal and her friends again. Why can't they leave me alone?

Mackie: What do you mean?

Sammy: They bother me every day. They are always teasing me about something. It's awful.

Fifth graders Crystal, Luis, and Jei come over to the peanut-free table.

Luis: I can't find my lunch box anywhere. I bet somebody stole it.

Jei: What color is it again?

Crystal: (*pointing at Sammy and Mackie*) Oh look at those little babies at the peanut table. Let's go say Hello!

Jei: Oh Crystal, don't bother those kids again.

Luis: Yeah, come on Crystal….

Crystal: Hello babies! How's life in kindergarten?

Mackie and Sammy try to ignore her.

Crystal: (*Looking at Sammy's lunch.*) OMG! What are you eating? Guys, look at this. Gross!

Luis: It looks better than my lunch.

Crystal: Are you kidding? It's disgusting!

(*Luis and Jei look at each other uncomfortably.*)

Crystal: I bet all of the food in your house is covered in mold!

(*Sammy covers his face and looks like he's about to cry. Mackie looks down at the floor.*)

Luis: Hey Crystal, why don't you leave them alone?

Crystal: What do you mean?

Jei: It's just not funny anymore.

Crystal: Well, if you don't think it's funny, why don't you go sit at the peanut table with the other babies?

Luis: I think I will! (*He goes to sit with Mackie and Sammy.*) Hey guys, wasn't that concert cool today?

Jei: (*Sees what Luis is doing and goes to sit at the peanut table too.*) Oh yeah, it was great! I hope I can be in the choir when I get to middle school.

(*Mackie and Sammy smile. Crystal is suddenly alone and looks uncomfortable and unhappy.*)

Crystal: Come on guys, you don't want to hang out with those kindergarten babies. Let's go…

Luis and Jei: No thanks!

Crystal: Oh whatever, I'm out of here. (*Crystal walks out.*)

Sammy: Thanks you guys!

Jei and **Luis:** No problem, buddy!!

The End

Reproducible Materials

In this section you will find reproducible handouts for your class.

1. **Diagram of Three Parts of the Brain**

2. **Conflict Resolution Toolbox**

3. **The Conflict CAT**

4. **The Conflict Escalator**

5. **Kindness Pals Template**

152 | | http://www.teachpeaceofmind.com

Diagram of Three Parts of the Brain

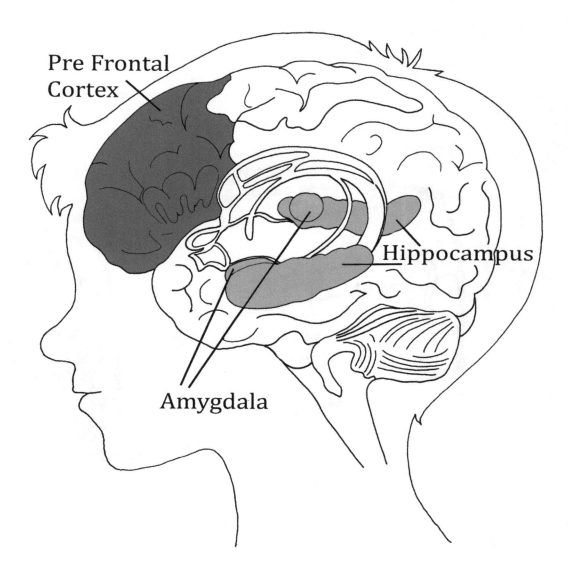

Pre Frontal Cortex

Hippocampus

Amygdala

The Conflict Toolbox

1. SHARE
2. TAKE TURNS
3. BE KIND
4. LEAVE IT TO CHANCE

5. COMPROMISE
6. PAUSE THE CONFLICT
7. SKIP THE CONFLICT
8. GET HELP

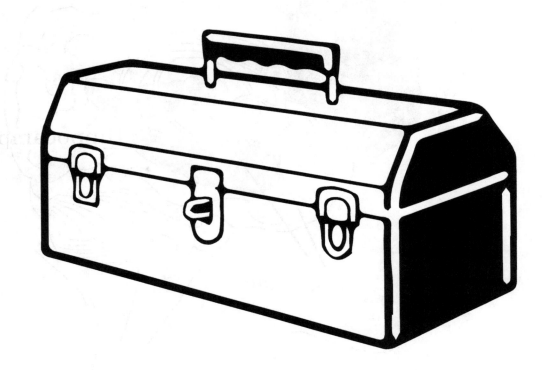

|

The Conflict CAT

The Conflict Escalator

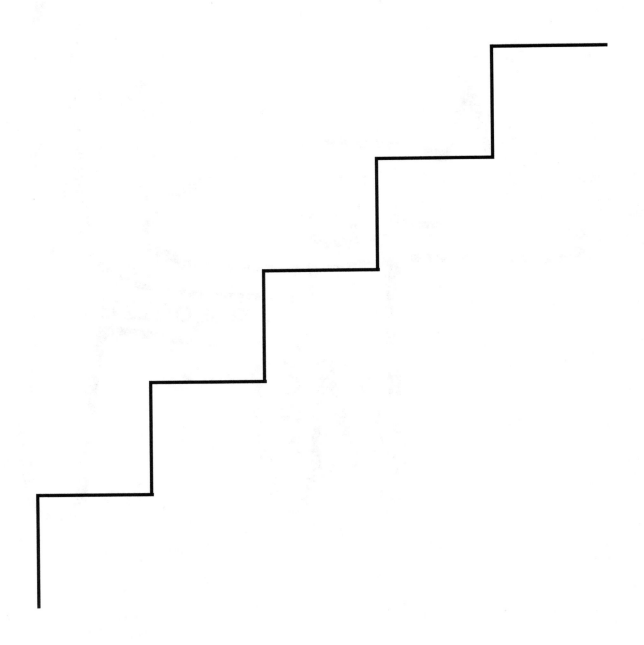

Kindness Pals List

for the week of _____

Student	Student
1.	
2.	
3.	
4.	
5.	
6.	
7.	
8.	
9.	
10.	
11.	
12.	
13.	
14.	
15.	

Peace of Mind

Materials for Lessons and Teachers

Books Used In Lessons

- <u>Enemy Pie</u> by Derek Munson
- <u>No Ordinary Apple</u> by Sara Marlowe
- <u>Rosie's Brain</u> by Linda Ryden
- <u>Say Something</u> by Peggy Moss
- <u>Sorry</u> by Trudy Ludwig
- <u>Steps and Stones</u> by Gail Silver
- <u>The Book of Awesome</u> by Neil Pasricha
- "The Zax" by Dr. Seuss in <u>The Sneetches and Other Stories</u>

Videos Used In Lessons

Just Breathe by Julia Bayer and Josh Saltzman <u>https://www.YouTube.com/watch?v=RVA2N6tX2cg</u>.

Rap by JusTme
<u>https://www.YouTube.com/watch?v=he-fw9_3egw</u>

Teacher Resources

Lesson Preparation
Daniel Siegel's Brain Talk Video (YouTube) <u>http://www.drdansiegel.com/resources/everyday_mindsight_tools/</u>

Teaching Mindfulness

Jennings, P. (2015). <u>Mindfulness for teachers: Simple skills for peace and productivity in the classroom</u>. The Norton Series on the Social Neuroscience of Education.

Minds Incorporated, <u>http://mindsincorporated.org/</u>

Mindful Schools, <u>http://www.mindfulschools.org/</u>

Rechtschaffen, D., & Kabat-Zinn PhD, J. (2014). <u>The Way of Mindful Education: Cultivating Well-being in Teachers and Students</u>. Norton Books in Education.

Personal Mindfulness Practice

Headspace.com

<u>Meditation Illuminated: Simple Ways to Manage Your Busy Mind</u> by Joy Rains

<u>Mindfulness: An Eight Week Plan for Finding Peace in a Frantic World</u> by Mark Williams and Danny Penman

Peace of Mind

Bibliography

Bradshaw, C. P. (2015). Translating research to practice in bullying prevention. *American Psychologist, 70* (4), 322-332.

Metz, S.M., Frank, J.L., Reibel, D., Cantrell, T., Sanders, R., & Broderick, P.C. (2013). The effectiveenss of Learning to BREATHE program on adolescent emotion regulation. *Research in Human Development, 10*(3), 252-272.

Lantieri, Linda. "How SEL and Mindfulness Can WorkTogether." Greater Good. April 7, 2015. Accessed September 28, 2015. http://greatergood.berkeley.edu/article/item/how_social_emotional_learning_and_mindfulness_can_work_together.

O'Brennan, L., & Bradshaw, C. (2013). School Climate: A Research Brief. A report prepared for the National Education Association, Washington, DC.

Schonert-Reichl, K. A., & Lawlor, M. S. (2010). The effects of a mindfulness-based education program on pre-and early adolescents' well-being and social and emotional competence. *Mindfulness, 1*(3), 137-151.

Weare, K. (2013). Developing mindfulness with children and young people: A review of the evidence and policy context. *Journal of Children's Services, 8*(2), 141-153.

Zoogman, S., Goldberg, S.B., Hoyt, W.T., & Miller, L. (2015). Mindfulness interventions with youth: A meta-analysis. *Mindfulness, 6*, 290 - 302.

Zenner, C., Hermleben-Kurz, S., & Walach, H. (2014). Mindfulness-based interventions in schools: A systematic review and meta-analysis. *Frontiers in Psychology, 5*, article 603.

Credits

Hand Model of the Brain. Lessons 14 and 42 "Everyday Mindsight Tools." Dr. Dan Siegel. March 17, 2011. Accessed September 28, 2015. http://www.drdansiegel.com/resources/everyday_mindsight_tools/

The Conflict Escalator. Lessons 28, 29, 31, 58-64 Kreidler, William J. *Teaching Conflict Resolution through Children's Literature*. New York: Scholastic Professional Books, 1994

Even if I come to Peace class sad or not feeling well or just in a bad mood, I always become very calm and happy by the end.

– Peace of Mind Student

Acknowledgements

Appreciation

My students have been my greatest teachers, my inspiration, and my joy. Each one of the more than 1,000 children I have worked with at Lafayette has taught me something important, and some have left lasting imprints on my heart. These children, some of who are in college now, fill me with hope that they will create a more peaceful world than the one they were born into.

In this testing-focused culture it takes courage to set aside time in the school day for something that can't be easily quantified. Many, many thanks to Lafayette Elementary Principal Dr. Carrie Broquard for her enthusiastic support for this program. Thanks to her leadership on this issue and willingness to go out on a limb, **Peace of Mind** has grown into an effective and engaging model program. Thanks also to former Lafayette Elementary School principal Lynn Main for her early support of the **Peace of Mind** program.

I owe a huge debt of gratitude to the wonderful teachers at Lafayette Elementary School who have welcomed and supported the **Peace of Mind** Program and given the very precious gift of classroom time. Many of the teachers at Lafayette have been on this journey with me from the very beginning and have trusted me with their students and given me their support when I needed it the most. Special thanks to my colleague Jared Catapano for taking up the challenge and becoming both a mindfulness teacher and, more importantly, a mindful teacher.

Lafayette Elementary's amazing School Counselor Jillian Diesner took on the challenge of adapting the **Peace of Mind** curriculum to our youngest students and has contributed so much of her expertise and creativity to expand Peace of Mind in wonderful new ways. Assistant Principal Jackie Snowden and School Counselor Rashida Mosby have been a constant source of support and encouragement.

Peace of Mind would not have been possible without the generous financial support of the Lafayette Home and School Association. Many thanks to all members, past and present, for supporting the program over the years, and for making our children's social emotional development a priority at Lafayette Elementary School.

I am grateful to the many people whose work inspires and informs **Peace of Mind.** Thank you to Annie Mahon for planting the very early seeds of the Peace program at Lafayette and for continuing to shine the light on Mindfulness.

From the very beginning Colman McCarthy, journalist and peace teacher, inspired me to follow my heart and teach peace. Thanks to Chris McKenna, Megan Cowan, and Vinnie Ferraro for inspired training and pioneering work in mindfulness education. Participating in their Mindfulness Fundamentals and Curriculum Trainings greatly enriched the Peace of Mind program. Thank you, too, to Professor Marsha Blakeway, whose expertise in conflict resolution and early encouragement made such a difference.

Thanks to Jesse Torrence, Dave Trachtenberg, and the Minds, Inc. family for bringing me into their fold and helping me to become part of the Mindfulness education movement. Your support and belief in me means the world.

This curriculum would never have happened without my Peace of Mind partner, Managing Editor, and friend, Cheryl Cole Dodwell. Cheryl offered wisdom, encouragement, organization, and heart to the writing of this curriculum and has been a long-time source of help and inspiration to me. I could never have done this without her generous commitment of time, expertise, and support.

My parents, John and Barbara Ryden were my first mindfulness role models. All of my life they have encouraged me to stop and enjoy the little things in life—from a beautiful song to a great meal to a wildflower to a ridiculous dog. Their gentle examples of kindness and ethical living have inspired me to do more with my life. They, along with my wise and creative aunt Katherine Ryden, offered their editorial expertise to the writing of this curriculum.

My dear sister, Tricia Ryden is a shining example of kindness and empathy. Her thoughtful editorial comments were crucial to the success of this curriculum.

My children, Rosie and Henry, continue to be my greatest pride and joy. They are the kindest people I know and fill me with hope for the future. My hard-working husband Jeremiah Cohen has given me endless support and encouragement in every way possible since the beginning of this journey. I couldn't have done this without the three of you.

With love and gratitude,

Linda Ryden
August 25, 2015

About Linda Ryden, Teacher and Author

Linda started teaching "Peace Class" in 2003 as a volunteer. Since then, her classes have grown into the **Peace of Mind** program which has become an integral part of the school curriculum and climate at Lafayette Elementary School in Washington DC. Now a full-time staff member at Lafayette, Linda works closely with school counselors, administrators and teachers and teaches the Peace of Mind Curriculum to over 500 students each week. Linda works with Minds, Inc. to train teachers in Mindfulness Education and consults with teachers and principals interested in creating Mindfulness and Social Emotional Learning programs in their own schools. Linda's work has been recognized in the Washington Post, the Huffington Post, and on CBS, ABC and Fox5 News.